GOOGIE MODERN

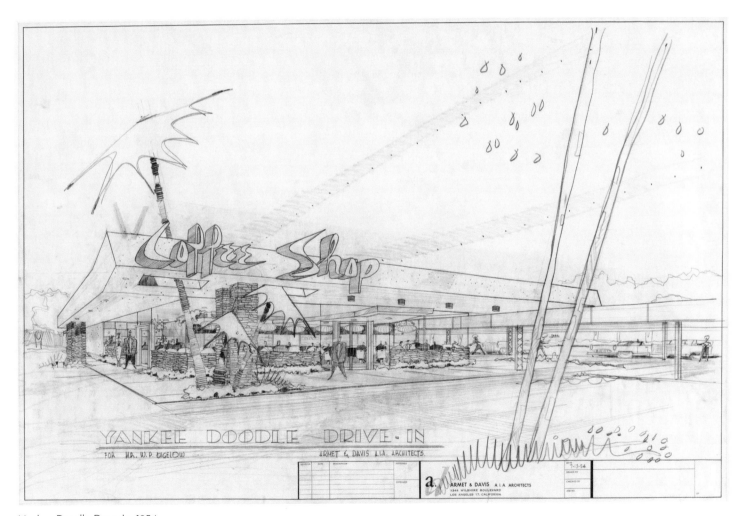

Yankee Doodle Drive-In, 1954

GOOGIE MODERN
ARCHITECTURAL DRAWINGS OF
ARMET DAVIS NEWLOVE

MICHAEL MURPHY
TEXT BY *ALAN HESS*
PHOTOGRAPHY BY *JENS LUCKING*

ANGEL CITY PRESS

Googie Modern: The Architectural Drawings of Armet Davis Newlove

By Michael Murphy

Copyright © 2022 by Michael Murphy. All rights reserved.

Introduction text, chapter text and captions copyright © 2022 by Alan Hess

Design by Michael Murphy

ISBN-13 978-1-62640-109-9

Library of Congress Cataloging-in-Publication Data is available.

ACP

ANGEL CITY PRESS

Published by Angel City Press

www.angelcitypress.com

Printed in Canada

Mel's Drive-In photographed by Jens Lucking

For Shannon Murphy, Cassidy Murphy, Jenson Lucking, Nicole Lucking, and Hamilton von Watts. - Michael Murphy

For Susan Snyder and George Thomas, carrying on the good work of Frank, Will, Bob, Denise, and Steve. - Alan Hess

CONTENTS

Hollys, Hawthorne, California, 1956

PREFACE /
MICHAEL MURPHY

Growing up in Santa Monica, California, I was fortunate enough to live on one of Southern California's great streets for diverse architecture, La Mesa Drive. Houses on this street were designed by some of the world's most renowned architects: Oscar Niemeyer, Paul R. Williams, John Byers, Elmer Grey, Lloyd Wright, H. Palmer Sabin, J.R. Davidson, and the firm of Marston, Van Pelt & Maybury.

My introduction to fine architecture was an unconscious one, a by-product of my endless neighborhood searches for places to jump my bike. Once I had been exposed to this wide range of architectural styles, however, I gradually began to feel the influence these spaces had on me. Granted, I was too young to appreciate many of these houses, like the one where I learned to roller-skate, designed by pioneering Black architect Paul R. Williams (please don't tell the Los Angeles Conservancy!). But I was aware enough of my surroundings to feel the energy and sensation of timeless aristocracy that emanates from that house into your body. One never forgets such a gift.

There were more benefits to growing up in Santa Monica; some came completely randomly. The first time I ditched school with my friend Eric Newlove was in 1986. I was thirteen, and we ended up at his parents' home, which was an unguarded fortress of art and architecture. Eric's father was Victor Newlove, he of the storied architecture firm Armet Davis Newlove (ADN), long famous for their mid-century restaurant designs. In addition to ADN sketches that were framed and hung on the walls, I saw a number of Julius Shulman photographs of Richard Neutra houses, fine art from some of North America's great artists, and a backyard full of kitschy sculptures, including a Bob's Big Boy statue and the "N" from a Norm's coffee shop sign. As a teenager, I didn't fully understand what I was looking at, but I was taken by it. The house was—and is—a special place. Whenever I found myself enjoying a meal at a late-night diner, I always thought about those giant, original drawings and quirky sculptures.

Fast-forward about thirty years to 2018. I'm at the Santa Monica History Museum, walking guests through my exhibit "Santa Monica: A Look Back to 1902 from Today"—based on my book of the same name—which features contemporary photos of the city overlaid on vintage photos of the same spots. I see Victor Newlove there and offer him a thirty-minute tour. As I'm walking him around, I'm reminded of his firm's architectural drawings, the same ones I stumbled upon while playing hooky as a kid. As we finish up, I decide then and there to pitch him the idea of a book based on the work of ADN.

Fortunately, he said yes.

That's when the real work began for me and my partner, photographer Jens Lucking. We were tasked with reproducing images of ADN's drawings from very thin, tightly rolled drafting paper that dated back as far as sixty years and contained sketches sometimes as large as four feet wide (and we had to make good on our promise to Mr. Newlove that we wouldn't damage the drafts). We sandwiched each drawing between two huge sheets of plastic to flatten them and get them camera ready. The work was all shot on-site at ADN's Santa Monica offices, where we had converted the meeting room into a huge light room. It was painstaking work: we wore white gloves to make sure these fragile works of art weren't damaged during handling. The effort was worth it, as we believe we conveyed the original works' sense of exuberance while ensuring the pieces were preserved.

Two years of immersion in Armet Davis Newlove's vast collection of drawings have left me with a deeper understanding of how different both Los Angeles and the country were when these projects were designed in the 1950s, 1960s, and 1970s. Evolving from the mid-century dream, ADN brought futurism, optimism, and hope to the everyday experience. Dining at an ADN-designed restaurant was more than just a meal; it fulfilled a social need for the typical American family to be a part of the post-war Modernism movement, one that fit right in with an affordable home, a new fast car, and a dream of space travel, topped off by a fresh cup of coffee.

As I continued my work, I recognized that Victor Newlove is "the keeper of the flame" of mid-century commercial architecture. Newlove worked and designed during the transition period between the primacy of diners and the expansion of fast-food chains. His work reflects a moment in which much about America was changing, and by carefully preserving the records of what he and his colleagues drew, we have been able to trace these shifts in time and place.

Jens Lucking converted the Armet Davis Newlove conference room in Santa Monica into a giant lightroom while photographing the original renderings.

We've included photographic overlays in this book that show where a building was erected—or was intended to be erected as a collective reminder of the power of these mid-century icons. Armet & Davis's vision became a mainstay in American culture, simply because their buildings shouted "Modern" to people who always demanded something new. As their idea of Modern aged, many buildings were torn down, the same way a family photo might be disregarded until rediscovered by a new generation. Like those family photos, a new generation is discovering Googie architecture, but at a time when it's almost too late. The photographic overlays in this book serve as a reminder of how much was lost—and how essential it will be to preserve what remains.

Mapping the Southern California locations of the ADN-designed restaurants that have been demolished also gave me a deeper perspective on the massive cultural shifts that occurred around the time that many of these restaurants were built, be they the massive expansion of the L.A. freeway system, the Watts Riots, or the flight of the middle class from the city to the suburbs. ADN's first restaurant, Clock, was built on a major thoroughfare that was once the primary route to Los Angeles International Airport. Today the site is an oil-changing station and fast-food drive-through on a street few use to get to LAX. Pix, a beautiful coffee shop on Western Avenue—a primary artery through the city—has been converted to a church. Architecture is no stranger to appropriation, and the story of these restaurants often tells of a wave of change that outpaced the advent of space travel.

Still, many of these buildings will live on forever in American pop culture. Ed Ruscha's painting *Norm's, La Cienega, On Fire* retains the same power in its depiction of the magnetic American roadside ethos that it did when it was created in 1964. The Hawthorne Grill (originally Holly's) served as the opening and closing backdrops for Quentin Tarantino's 1994 genre-defying film classic, *Pulp Fiction*. For Tarantino, the coffee shop's open interior space and vast windows reinforced his film's message that American freedom and American chaos are players in the same scene and probably even eat in adjoining vinyl booths every day. Ruscha's flames on his coffee shop act not only to "torch" American norms and standards, according to art critic Michael Darling, but also to celebrate and illuminate these norms. Both Tarantino and Ruscha use Googie style to depict the complicated notion of Americana being two things at once: a mirror of the possible and the repressed. It just depends on how you see yourself, and how you see the person sitting at the next table.

There is no question as to who was the "typical" diner these designers had in mind in the 1950s and 1960s—surely the white, middle-class male. But I prefer to look at whom these restaurants serve today and how an architecture of optimism reaches all Americans. Case in point: Los Angeles's Wich Stand, built on a hilltop in a white neighborhood in 1957 and described by the Beach Boys as a hangout and hot-rodders' paradise for privileged suburban kids. Shuttered in 1988, the building reopened in 1995 as Simply Wholesome, a thriving vegan restaurant that serves the largely African American communities of Ladera Heights and Baldwin Hills. That is a great Googie story. A great L.A. story. A great American story.

Of course, not all of these buildings vanished silently or only live on as lost pop-culture symbols. Many keep the Googie flame alive. ADN-designed restaurants such as Pann's and Astro Family Restaurant (originally Conrad's) remain family-owned Los Angeles institutions. Denny's, born in Southern California in 1955, has since taken the Googie ethos worldwide. And though the Hawthorne Grill was torn down in 1999 (there's an AutoZone in its place), Norm's La Cienega is alive and well. And not on fire.

Norm's, La Cienega, on Fire, Ed Ruscha, 1964 (© Ed Ruscha)

THE VIEW FROM THE WINDSHIELD
/ INTRODUCTION
ALAN HESS

For the price of a hamburger or a tuna melt, ordinary Angelenos could be a part of the future at any Googie coffee shop.

Once they stepped out of their DeSoto or Mercury, pulled open the custom-designed ceramic door pull that could have been a piece of Modern art, and sat down on a cantilevered counter stool, they could survey the selection of pies in the stainless-steel glass-fronted case overhead while a waitress in a crisp uniform—coordinated in the style and color of the coffee shop—strolled over to take their order.

Detail; Woody Holder's Sierra Inn Restaurant, c. 1955

This scene would be repeated in a thousand ways every day in the 1950s and 1960s. It might be a different car or a different meal, and the coffee shop might be named Pix, Holly's, Ships, or Bob's, but each scene belonged to the same moment in American time. After 1945, a string of newly built coffee shops, soon to be labeled "Googie architecture," sprang up on the commercial strips of the new suburbs of Los Angeles, the San Fernando Valley, the San Gabriel Valley, Orange County, and San Diego. This was the California coffee shop—a new type of restaurant with a new architecture that was a space age beyond the diners refashioned from old railroad cars that dotted the East Coast.

These new eateries spread quickly to Arizona, Texas, Illinois, Michigan, Florida, and beyond. The times conjured them. Most American garages now held at least one car; those vehicles had inspired the redesigning of the city in the image of its newly mobile population. The ancient prototype city designed by Le Corbusier's donkey was being replaced by the motorist's city of sleek, speedy thoroughfares lined with sparkling glass walls and neon signs.

Googie reigned on these boulevards, in the form of coffee shops, gas stations, car washes, bowling alleys, motels, and car

dealerships. These structures were descended from a long line of giant derbies, oranges, pumpkins, and Streamline Moderne drive-ins from the 1920s and 1930s that were the first to acknowledge how the motorist lived in this new age. Industrial designer Norman Bel Geddes heralded them as symbols of modern times as much as the talkies and vaudeville era. When the post-World War II economic and population booms injected new energy into the design of roadside businesses, Southern California's Modern architects picked up the ball and carried these ideas even further.

Teddy's Drive-in, 1955

Vividly designed and plugged into the currents of American life and culture, Googie quickly became a referent in both high and popular culture. The namesake Googies coffee shop became the Sunset Strip hangout for James Dean, Marilyn Monroe, Elvis Presley, and a host of young, hip actors. Decades later, in the movies, Quentin Tarantino saw the value of Googie style as a setting for his film *Pulp Fiction* (1994), as did the Coen brothers for *The Big Lebowski* (1998) and David Lynch for *Mulholland Drive* (2001). The architecture in the animated Pixar films *The Incredibles* (2004) and *Incredibles 2* (2018) drew heartily from Googie, outdoing even the futuristic vision of Hanna-Barbera's TV cartoon classic *The Jetsons* (1962-1963), which was produced well after Googie architecture had become common on Los Angeles streets, especially around the Hanna-Barbera headquarters in the San Fernando Valley. Creator Matthew Weiner chose authentic Googie locations for *Mad Men* (2007-2015) to complement the High Modern offices of the show's advertising firm of Sterling Cooper Draper Pryce. As an even more pointed testament to Googie's cultural impact,

Weiner wrote the first draft of the popular series at none other than Norm's La Cienega.

In professional and high-art culture, Douglas Haskell, editor for Henry Luce's *House & Home* magazine, introduced the term "Googie" to a professional audience in a 1952 article. Giving the phenomenon a label allowed people to identify it as it began cropping up everywhere. New Journalist Tom Wolfe, in the 1960s, recognized Googie sites as premier design salons of the youth culture for clothes, hair, cars, and architecture. Artist Ed Ruscha saw the power of illustrating one aflame in *Norm's, La Cienega, On Fire* (1964). Keen-eyed British observer Reyner Banham discussed the style alongside Rudolph Schindler, Richard Neutra, and the Case Study Houses in his seminal 1971 book, *Los Angeles: The Architecture of Four Ecologies.*

The architecture of Googie drew deeply from these cultural currents. Southern California's up-and-coming architects, after all, lived among cars, suburbs, drive-ins, and Los Angeles's innovations accommodating the rise of the automobile. Lloyd Wright's 1928 drive-in market at Yucca and Vine, in the center of Hollywood, had distilled the concepts that would later be called Googie: a roadside business for car-mobile citizens, convenient parking, a tall pylon to direct attention, a distinct roofline, and nighttime illumination, all rendered in stylishly modern materials. Soon after, architect Wayne McAllister applied the same concepts to the drive-in restaurants that were spreading across the southland; most major intersections seemed to have at least one. In quick succession—now that peace had arrived following the end of the war in 1945—restaurateurs caught the wave. William "Tiny" Naylor hired architect Douglas Honnold to design a drive-in coffee shop at the Hollywood intersection of Sunset and La Brea that was half drive-in, half rocket plane. Businessman Mort Burton hired architect John Lautner to design Googies, the Sunset Strip restaurant whose spectacularly original design would lend its name to the entire phenomenon. Lautner understood this new urban energy and, liberated and guided by his education under Frank Lloyd Wright, gave it a form like no other—enough to cause Haskell, who had been driving through West Hollywood researching the emergence of these flashy eateries, to bring his car to a screeching halt.

Feeling no pressure to please East Coast critics, Southern

California's architects recognized this architecture's potential and quickly embraced it for their clients and customers. Some, like Armet & Davis and Martin Stern Jr., were solid commercial architects solving their clients' problems with creative pragmatism. Others, including Lautner, A. Quincy Jones, Palmer & Krisel, William F. Cody, Douglas Honnold, Smith & Williams, and Russell Forester, were already respected by high-art critics for their notable Modern residential designs but also saw coffee shops, car dealerships, and drive-ins as equally legitimate challenges for Modern architects to solve. Together, these architects created a remarkably unified landscape for the new kind of city planned and designed around suburban lifestyles and the technological possibilities of the automobile. The high quality of all of their designs renders any distinction between "high art" and "commercial" architects inconsequential, no matter how many critics insisted on distinguishing them.

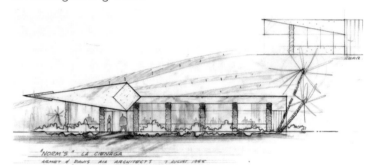

Norm's #4 La Cienega (Prototype), 1955

Notice, for example, the glass walls that the famous Case Study House #22 (Pierre Koenig, 1960) shares with Norm's La Cienega (Armet & Davis, 1954). Critics at the time did not. A modern technology (large sheets of plate glass) is used in both buildings to connect interior and exterior, to diminish the traditional barrier dividing a sheltered human habitat from the climate outside. Julius Shulman's celebrated nighttime photo of Case Study #22 is all about the glass and what it allows in this astonishing modern building. That is the same role performed by Norm's glass wall from six years before. The only difference is that the Case Study House's glass walls lie at the rear of the house, uniting the distant city panorama with the living space and turning a blank wall to the street (an homage to Frank Lloyd Wright's Usonian homes). Norm's, however, turns its enormous glass wall to the immediate public street, exploiting the possibilities of glass to embrace the urban scene and unite it with the dining space.

Both are effective and, at the time, startling uses of glass in architecture. Critics praised the residential use, but overlooked the equally innovative commercial design.

Note how often the name of Frank Lloyd Wright crops up in this architectural genealogy. Through Wright, Louis Sullivan, and Frank Furness, Organic architecture (a major current in Modern design) took root in America long before Europe's mechanistic Bauhaus Modernism was born. From these American roots, the intentional balancing of modern technology and autochthonous nature is visible in Googie architecture's contrast of high-tech roof structures aloft on natural stone pillars that rise from lush landscaping. Googie resolves the tension between the artificial and the natural. Wright himself anticipated this fruitful direction when he moved to the Sunbelt in the mid-1930s. Armet & Davis would continue this conceptual thread by contrasting sleek steel, glass, and high-tech engineering with natural landscaping and materials. Though they followed in the tradition of Organic Modernism, they advanced those concepts, reinterpreting and applying them to the new culture of the car and the suburban city.

Yet, in spite of l'esprit nouveau radiating from the coffee shops frequented every day by Southern Californians, these iconic structures have been largely excluded from that history. You'd be hard-pressed to find a positive reference to Googie in most histories until the end of the century. Future Yale architecture chair Paul Rudolph confessed in 1952 to a "fear of producing 'googie' architecture if the disciplines of the ages" were not observed when the imagination was unleashed. To many critics, Googies coffee shops seemed exaggerated, cartoonish. They were assumed to be a lesser Modernism simply for being commercial, rather than a "pure" architecture of home, church, or museum—gentlemanly commissions for the educated, not buildings for the rough-and-tumble of daily life. (Never mind that two seminal turning points in Modernism—skyscraper offices and functional factories—were both profoundly commercial in nature.) Googie kowtowed to the needs of the auto a little too imaginatively, critics suspected. They were tarnished simply as a product of Los Angeles; while the city's elegant residences of the Case Study House Program for Arts & Architecture magazine landed safely within the boundaries of the sanctioned

International Style, the swoops, shapes, colors, and car-culture provenance of these Wrightian coffee shops were well outside the lines. They were not Architecture with a capital A.

Or so we have been told.

Slowly we're learning otherwise. Googie is a chapter in the larger story of the evolution of Modern architecture. The drawings collected in this book are part of the proof. They reside in the archives of Armet Davis Newlove, the most prolific mid-century architecture firm designing Googie architecture across North America. Modern design results from the expression of functions rather than historic precedents. Googie defined new dimensions of Modernism; today it compels us to reassess how we judge Modern architecture. Like all Modern architecture, Googie uses and expresses twentieth-century technology—notably the auto, engineering, and the urbanism and lifestyles they brought into existence. Technology created a spirit of optimism: any problem could be solved, so it seemed. In Googie's primary period (roughly 1945–1975), responding to the auto-oriented suburban life with a convenient and practical design, and deriving new forms and methods of expressing and reflecting these new functions.

Frisch's Big Boy Coffee Shop & Drive-In, 1957

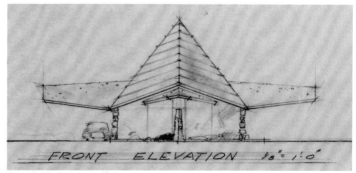

Detail; Plush Pup Self-Service Restaurant, c. 1960

Detail; Huddle Restaurant #4 (Study), 1954

Googie expanded the concept of Modernism in three significant ways: it is fundamentally democratic as part of the daily life of the average person; it enthusiastically incorporates pleasure in its designs; and it is an architecture of modern communication.

Googie's expansive glass walls, combined with air-conditioning, evoked the environment of outdoor patio dining (one of the pleasures of Southern California living) surrounded by subtropical landscaping and the glinting, kinetic, ever-changing panorama of the commercial strip. Interiors offered a selection of seating, from counter stools (where you were entertained watching the cooks prepare your meal), to tables with Eames chairs, to banquettes and booths in quieter areas of the restaurant. It was Modern space—not the right-angled box of International Style Modernism, but a flowing, complex space that curved around corners and connected indoors and outdoors through glass walls.

With the bold scale of their rooflines, their billboard-size glass walls, and their integrated neon signs, Googie buildings are the architecture of modern communication. Earlier in the century, George Howe and William Lescaze insisted on crowning their 1932 Philadelphia Savings Fund Society skyscraper, built in the International Style, with an enormous neon sign bearing the initials "PSFS" visible across the metropolis. The Constructivists, another group of Modernists in the early former Soviet Union, also integrated sign and architecture: their buildings could convey messages through form, signage, electronics, or siting. Modern techniques use advertising billboards, animated signage, loudspeakers, and neon to broadcast a message. Later in the century, this aspect of Modern architecture would be picked up by Times Square, the Ginza, Las Vegas, and Los Angeles; Googie was a particularly creative and successful expression of the architecture of modern communication.

Projecting a structure's purpose, location, and character was a key concept in Googie design. Building on the earlier exploration of manipulating scale and image with giant derbies, dogs, and tamales, Armet & Davis learned to integrate those concepts into structure and roof forms. The roof itself served as an abstract canvas for broadcasting the building's presence on a busy commercial strip site. It may have seemed exaggerated to some critics, but it was the appropriate scale to be legible to a motorist driving by at 40 mph. The glass wall stretching across the entire facade was an eye-catching three-dimensional billboard, showing off its product in a bright, colorful tableau of happy customers.

The materials were the message too: glass, open-webbed I-beam columns, colorful mosaics and Formica veneers, stainless-steel cabinetry, rugged Palos Verdes stone, pulsating fonts, animated neon, FlagCrete masonry, and Modern art

and ornament all conveyed the excitement and optimism of the times. Appealing to a broad cross section of the population, the style was in tune with current popular taste, which, in 1950s L.A., meant an optimistic view of modern life and technology.

A sign on a pole—freestanding, angled, or piercing the dramatic roof—often complemented the shape of the roof to create a total design. The sign was usually animated neon, another modern technology. Often, the very letters of the coffee shop's name were melded into the structure itself, at large scale and in three dimensions. The sign became the architecture, the architecture became the sign—a sophisticated architectural concept that Robert Venturi, Denise Scott Brown, and Steven Izenour would later identify in their famous treatise, Learning from Las Vegas (1972). Googie played a major role in evolving this concept.

Detail; Carolina Pines Jr. Restaurant (Concept), 1955

Detail; Mar Vista Bowl (Concept), 1959

Though democracy and sometimes pleasure received lip service in Modernist manifestos, Googie's radical expression of them was nearly impossible for critics to recognize. Almost in spite of himself, eminent historian Henry-Russell Hitchcock had been impressed by an example in 1940 (a Van de Kamp's drive-in and coffee shop defined by the chain's trademark windmill), describing it as "a very model of what exposition or resort architecture ought to be, light, gay, open, well executed.... Nothing in the East compares with the best things of this sort in Los Angeles." Yet, he also presumed that its design was the random result of an "effectively anonymous" vernacular process.

No, it wasn't.

Architect Wayne McAllister, with offices in Los Angeles, had designed it and a series of superb Streamline Moderne drive-ins in the 1930s, the most explicit and farsighted examples of Modern architecture anywhere in the world at the time. They were the immediate predecessors of post-war Googie. Using the modern materials of steel and neon, their circular forms and tall, neon-lit pylons were determined by the turning radius of autos and the efficiency of carhop food service. More than that, they suited the lifestyles of a population that ate, watched movies, bought groceries, and generally lived in their cars. As much as steel, glass, or concrete, the automobile was the technology that refashioned architecture.

As a result of critics' neglect and disrespect for this democratic and commercial Los Angeles architecture, many if not most Googie buildings have been remodeled, poorly maintained, or demolished over the decades. The drawings in this book, however, open a broad window onto the original concepts their architects intended. These drawings make the freshness of their designs, the modernity of their functions, and the energy and vitality of their commercial-strip setting in new suburban metropolises vividly obvious.

The lessons of these designs help us expand what Modern architecture was, is, and can be. They help us redefine how we measure it by acknowledging its popular purposes and styles. Historians and tastemakers have trained us to see great design as the product of a prophetic genius (a Frank Lloyd Wright, a Zaha Hadid) who sees all, knows all, and bestows form on the future. But more often, important architecture emerges as the riptides of culture, economics, technology, and history collide and quick-witted architects take advantage of the disruption left in their wake. Effective solutions evolve over time, owing to the contributions of many architects and builders, some famous and some less so. Mining such vernacular resources is one of American culture's great strengths. This is the process that makes vernacular architecture so successful and a rich source of inspiration to good architects; factories, skyscrapers, mass-produced housing, neon signs, and roadside restaurants are a few examples. In mid-century Southern California, the vernacular culture of the car thrived at the grassroots level in the customized hot rod. These were design objects any kid might imagine building—or, at least, imagine cruising the Strip in one and stopping at a Googies coffee shop, as Tom Wolfe documented in his 1968 essay "The Hair Boys."

Googie turns out to be an essential chapter in the history of Modern architecture. It democratizes the style, convenience, and benefits of Modern design and theory. Its concepts and realizations broaden the way architecture should be measured today, and its creative use of vernacular roots and pragmatic commercial functions is as important as its references to high-art sources. At its core, Googie's embrace of pleasure and delight must be respected because of its very success.

All for the price of a hamburger or a tuna melt.

Detail; Pix Coffee Shop, 1956

Detail; Frisch's Big Boy Coffee Shop, 1962

THE ARMET & DAVIS OFFICE
/ 1947-1974

Louis Armet and Eldon Davis met as students at the University of Southern California School of Architecture in the late 1930s. Armet (1914-1981) graduated in 1939, Davis (1917-2011) in 1942. At the time, USC was one of the foremost architecture schools in the country teaching Modernism; its faculty would include Richard Neutra, Calvin Straub, William Pereira, Whitney Smith, and Craig Ellwood. William Cody, Frank Gehry, William Krisel, and Richard Dorman, as well as Davis and Armet, who are among alumni who have distinguished the school.

Though the USC architecture school is known for pioneering the elegant post-and-beam style, the Googie architecture espoused by alumni Armet, Davis, Cody, and Krisel was equally original and influential in defining Modernism. Springs Coffee Shop in Palm Springs, visualized by Cody, and Coffee Dan's in Van Nuys, designed by Krisel, did justice to the genre. True, coffee shops were not considered the prestigious architectural commissions that houses were. Yet, time after time, in the sketches we see here for Googies downtown coffee shop, the Hot Shoppes, or Romeo's Times Square, Armet & Davis designs extend the rich natural textures, engineering exuberance, and appreciation of color, pattern, and ornament that became hallmarks of the Modern tradition in America, from Frank Furness to Louis Sullivan to Frank Lloyd Wright to John Lautner.

After USC, Louis Armet and Eldon Davis became partners in 1947. Their early years were aided by Armet's connections to Los Angeles's Catholic diocese. In addition to churches, schools, and rectories, the firm's projects included offices, custom-designed houses, retail stores, nurseries, an auto repair shop, a laundromat, exhibition buildings, fire stations, and markets. Several of these types of buildings became mainstays of the firm for decades. Armet & Davis also took on numerous remodels, including interior alterations to the original Googies restaurant designed by John Lautner. The partners divided the work, each leading his own office projects: Armet concentrated on schools and church buildings, while Davis took on most of the coffee shops, which became a major part of their business. In 1951, the commission for a new building for Clock

restaurants unexpectedly launched the firm in a direction that would expand the very definition of Modernism in new and controversial ways. The client, Forest Smith, would continue to bring in steady work for the firm.

Eldon Davis (left) and Louis Armet with a model of a Huddle Restaurant designed for Pasadena, c. 1954.

As business grew, Davis and Armet sought out young, enthusiastic talent much like themselves. Richard Dorman (1922-2010) arrived at the offices in 1950. A year later, he became director of design at Welton Becket Associates before going on to establish his own firm and a national reputation for innovative design. Another hire, Pat DeRosa, later founded the firm of Powers, Daly & DeRosa, which was responsible for the popular Googie-style bowling alleys across the nation.

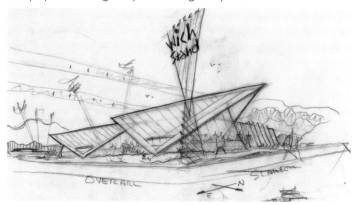

The Wich Stand, 1957

But perhaps Armet & Davis's most significant associate was Helen Liu Fong (1927-2005), who started as a draftsperson in 1951. She would become a key designer, remaining with the firm until the late 1970s. Back in the early 1950s, the contributions to architecture of women and of designers of Asian descent were often not noted in articles and histories. Bucking the system, Fong—both a woman and a person of Asian descent—became a valued colleague in the Armet & Davis offices, where she helped to define Googie architecture. Her father, an immigrant, moved with his family to Los Angeles, where Helen was born. There, the entire family helped run their laundry business. Graduating with a degree in city planning from the school of architecture at the University of California, Berkeley, in 1949, Fong returned to Los Angeles and worked for architect Eugene Choy (Armet's classmate at USC), then joined Armet & Davis, whose offices were in the same building. In 1964, she became an associate in charge of client relationships, interior decor, and restaurant projects. Though she did not personally draw these renderings, she worked closely with other staff in realizing them. Her hand is evident in many of the projects presented in this book.

Around the time Fong joined the firm, Lee Linton (1922-2006) came on as a designer and renderer who would have a major impact on the offices' direction. The 1952 Huddle La Cienega study drawings [pages 42-43] are the first documented evidence of Linton's work. So detailed were his drawings that they became critical tools in developing the architecture, its scale, and the relation of interior to exterior. Beyond that, the noisy, happy exuberance of Linton's drawings captured the essence of Googie: energetic, popular, and, above all, Modern in style, temperament, and delight.

Victor Newlove (b. 1941), another important figure at Armet & Davis, started in 1963 as a summer intern. By 1972, he was a partner in what was renamed Armet Davis Newlove. His affinity for Googie architecture, however, had begun much earlier. As a child growing up in Santa Monica, he was transfixed by the design of the Huddle Santa Monica restaurant by Armet & Davis. After interning at the firm, he graduated from the School of Architecture at Notre Dame University in 1964. He returned to Armet & Davis, where he worked on his own projects, but also worked with two other exceptional Modernist Los Angeles firms, Thornton Abell and Jones & Emmons. Newlove was particularly influenced by the graphic style of architect Kazuo Nomura, who helped create Jones & Emmons's signature presentation style.

THE DRAWINGS

Two primary categories of drawings are included in this collection: study sketches (both freehand and hard lined) used to develop design ideas, and formal presentation drawings made for clients. The study sketches—especially those done by Linton—allow us to enter into the mind of the designer. They highlight the buildings' best features, their settings in the city, and the ways in which happy customers would enjoy them. Often they were done at an impressively large scale (3 by 4 feet); looking at, say, a rendering of a restaurant, you feel you could walk right in and sit down. Sometimes they were drawn by the lead designer, as in the case of Linton, or by others under the direction of the lead architect. Along with, at times, scale models, the drawings served as design tools to approximate as closely as possible the character of the finished building.

Romeo's Times Square Restaurant, 1955

Design is, of course, a collaborative effort. At Armet & Davis, Eldon Davis was the partner in charge, giving guidance based on the evolving drawings. In later years, presentation drawings were more often made by professional renderers once the design had been approved. This process of modern commercial design parallels that for automakers in Detroit, where stylists would create drawings or build clay models of new cars in order to study the effectiveness of their designs.

Large presentation works started as line drawings in pencil. A straightedge such as a T-square would be used, or they would be drawn loosely by hand, which helped the designer work out ideas as they drew. Once the large-format rendering was finished, it would be made into a blueprint or photographed for further reproductions where color would be added. Occasionally, colored pencils or grease pencils would be used on the original rendering or study sketches.

The full character, formal play, and sheer forcefulness of the study sketches were drawn from the cacophonous, humming, active environment of the new suburban commercial strips—and from the role these designs played in bringing order and focus to that modern tumult. Linton's sketch for Mel's suggests this [page 151]. With its curving roof, the drawing embodies the bold swagger of Modern thinking: like a gymnast's performance, dynamic thrust is balanced by solid counterweight. The seemingly impossible extension of the cantilevered roof is made visually believable by the anchoring concrete-block rear. This concept would later be repeated in the Bob's Big Boy prototype of 1960 [page 126].

Mel's Coffee Shop, 1957

Though renderings of Googie buildings can appear exaggerated, the buildings in situ often share the character Linton captured in his drawings. His designs are rife with detail: the oval pattern at the rear of Mel's shows how the functional material of concrete block also has the ability to play dress-up, with bas-relief ornamentation catching sunlight and shadow. The scalloped horizontal roofline is echoed by the vertical lettering, integrating sign and structure; a galaxy of can lights in the ceiling brings the interior to life at night, when the window wall seems to disappear and the glowing, colorful interior, filled with customers, transforms into a three-dimensional billboard for the diner. As in so many of the Armet & Davis drawings, the building is rooted in its environmental context: the boulevard stretching to the horizon, cars whizzing by, palm trees placed as vertical accents to the building design, wispy clouds floating across the blue Southern California sky.

From the subdued yet clear presentation of the Clock drawing a few years earlier, Armet & Davis had grown confident about Modern expression in their design and the rendering style. They arrived at the appropriate and necessary architectural solution to the suburban car-culture program they were innovating. The drawings are key elements of their design process.

Before modern computer-aided simulation, hand-drawn architectural renderings played a large role in defining and popularizing styles over the years. Claude-Nicolas Ledoux's eighteenth-century renderings of solemn cenotaphs conveyed the grandeur that he intended. Marion Mahony Griffin was instrumental in communicating the relationship between Frank Lloyd Wright's designs and their natural context, as well as their intentional evocation of Japanese art. Hugh Ferriss's scenographic black-and-white depictions exaggerated and highlighted Modern architecture's urban drama.

Acting in concert, Armet & Davis's contemporaries in Los Angeles used hand-rendered drawings as a tool to refine and convey their concepts. A modern technique developed for Modern architecture, it was spread by architectural journals. Eschewing the lithographic realism of Beaux-Arts, the practice instead adopted a freer, abstract style echoing modern art and graphics and using striking new elements such as cutaway sections and startling perspectives. Ralph Rapson's drawing of his Greenbelt Case Study design (never built but made famous by his drawing) placed the viewer in the sky, looking down on a husband as he returns home in a helicopter and waves to his wife and kids on the ground below. Jones & Emmons's illustrations by Kazuo Nomura, Larry Thompson, Louis J. Liets, Donald Boss, and A. Quincy Jones himself were equally careful to set the Modern stage for their buildings through distinct renderings. Another architect and consummate renderer, William Krisel, used his own pen to make and sell designs to clients while engaging himself in the process of creation. In the catalog accompanying the Getty Museum's 2013 Pacific Standard Time exhibit, curator Wim de Wit noted that "Krisel's drawings...show a total joy of producing the drawing...a feeling of excitement." Armet & Davis's renderings do as well.

This assertively modern graphic style is also evident in the work of Los Angeles graphic artists and animators of the period. Graphic artist Alvin Lustig (who often collaborated with local architects on signage and architecture) and designer

Alexander Girard (who worked with Ray and Charles Eames) used similar modern abstraction, often adapting the Cubism, Impressionism, and Surrealism of contemporary fine artists. Such a transition was also led by animators Chuck Jones and Friz Freleng at the Warner Bros. studio, and by Jay Ward Productions and United Productions of America. Even Walt Disney Productions abandoned the lush, painstakingly drawn graphic style of Pinocchio and Snow White and the Seven Dwarfs for the colorful, impressionist palette of Peter Pan and Cinderella, guided by animator Ward Kimball and artists Mary Blair and Eyvind Earle. It was no coincidence that these influential companies were all based in Los Angeles, and not far from the offices of Armet & Davis.

The firm's rendering style used by Linton and others proved an ideal match for the coffee shops. A sense of free-spirited whimsy and delight—rarely associated with the professional seriousness of many Modern architects—may have been one reason critics did not take Googie seriously, but was proof that architecture was becoming more democratic, more appealing to the general audience, and more focused on improving the architecture of daily life.

Selective abstraction, conveyed through Linton's deft use of line weight, simplified the outline of buildings, vegetation, cars, and people to train the viewer's eye on the most important elements. Dramatic perspectives of the long commercial strip setting added the energy of movement to the point of view, much as Richard Neutra did in renderings of his idealistic vision of transportation, Rush City. Linton's drawings show the perspective of the motorist's eye as it tracks down the street, taking in the dense visual information of the surrounding commercial strip, with the manifestation of the coffee shop rising irresistibly to capture one's attention. These structures served as orienting landmarks, much like church steeples in nineteenth-century New England. By freezing a moment in time, as in a photograph, the drawings communicated how the building would be utilized by people walking in, sitting at counters, or ordering from a carhop. Lofty palms, flowering yuccas, and spiky aloes (appropriate to the Mediterranean climate) are not afterthoughts but intentional parts of the composition, adding vertical elements to frame the horizontal ones. Rich, artfully composed textures highlighted materials, structure, landscaping, paving, even the natural setting of sky and clouds. The common thread among them was a wit that

made these drawings relatable to the general public in a way that didactic, avant-garde Modern architectural renderings did not. These drawings and buildings were intended to be popular.

Carolina Pines Jr. Restaurant (Concept), 1955

Linton created a sense of dimensionality almost like that of a cinematic tracking shot. In a single work, he transports the viewer from a wide shot of the broad urban panorama, through the front door, and into close-ups of customers dining at counters. The atmospheric decor is rendered as carefully as the overall structure: lighting fixtures, soffits, and original artwork draw the eye deep into the interior space. His drawings tell the story not of an isolated building but of the people and daily life whirling through and around it. However abstract, these are real buildings—not cartoons, not advertising eyewash. As hyperbolic as some of Linton's drawings may appear, the experience of the actual buildings frequently harbors the same dramatic presence. Not only were these drawings an effective means of selling a client on a design, but they also expressed Modern architectural concepts.

Armet & Davis's coffee shops are as much a part of the car-culture art that emerged in Los Angeles in the 1950s as Billy Al Bengston's Finish Fetish paintings, George Barris's customized cars, Harley Earl's sweep-spears, and Von Dutch's pinstriping. This diverse design culture created a remarkable aesthetic that connected the car dashboard to the coffee shop counter. It was the essence of Los Angeles at the time, spanning high art in galleries and popular art on the street, the art of the auto made by kids tinkering with hot rods in garages and by manufacturers in Detroit. In his essays "Electrographic Architecture" and "The Hair Boys," Tom Wolfe cataloged the fashions, cars, and buildings he presents as part of an advancing cultural tsunami in the form of Southern California's drive-ins and coffee shops.

Huddle Restaurant (Proposal), 1954

By The Number, 1963

All of this can be detected in Armet & Davis's designs and Linton's drawings. The sinuous, pulsating fonts (invented for each coffee shop) on signs—thrusting out in three dimensions—capture the same rich, artistic atmosphere. Vivid mixes and contrasts of materials, shapes, textures, and patterns generate an eclectic energy that sets Organic and popular Modernism apart from the minimalism of International Style Modernism. Linton's specialty of featuring stylish women in couture fashions and men in plaid sports jackets are not afterthoughts but part of the design aesthetic.

Linton left the firm in 1959 to obtain his architecture license and start his own office in Las Vegas. His rendering style had influenced other architects in the office, who succeeded in capturing the same narrative energy and modern abstraction. One, however, brought his own distinguished style. Trained at Carnegie Tech in Pittsburgh, Don Hocker imbued his renderings with a clean, descriptive, professional quality. While not as exuberantly idiosyncratic as Linton's, Hocker's drawings

nevertheless exuded the wit and personality that breathed life into these buildings.

In the 1960s, Armet & Davis hired professional architectural renderers such as Alfred M. Gordon and Robert Jackson, and professional artists such as Siegfried Knop and Toby Nippel (a noted automotive artist) who did renderings on the side. Drawing styles vary and take on a softer approach to line weight, presenting calmer images. For example, realism dominates the rendering of Biff's coffee shop [page 187], resulting in a shapely, colorful view with naturalistically proportioned customers walking away after a satisfying meal.

THE BUILDINGS

Clock (1951), Armet & Davis's first coffee shop [page 36–37], was a worthy initial design. In it we can see early iterations of the concepts that would coalesce into their 1954 Norm's design as the classic Googie style. The drawing itself exhibits a tentative, just-the-facts-ma'am style, yet it proclaims the fundamental DNA of Googie-to-be: the enormous red sign is an arrow, a dynamic directional form that makes the building at one with the rhythmic energy of L.A. commercial strips. The sweeping "C" in "Clock" arrests the eye and draws it inside. Piercing through the long glass facade and slicing into the flat roof, the triangular sign is echoed in the window frames and slanting end walls, unifying the entire design. It is an intentionally non-rectilinear, non-International Style geometry aligned with Wright's triangular/hexagonal/circular geometries, and well suited to Los Angeles.

The success of the Clock design soon drew Armet & Davis into the post-war restaurant industry boom in Southern California. Like many other firms, they produced a steady stream of public buildings, private homes, and civic buildings. But with Clock, followed by Huddle on La Cienega's swank Restaurant Row and Chefs Inn farther south, they earned a reputation for designing successful restaurants. In contrast to Clock, Chefs Inn was an upscale dining establishment; residential in scale, it fit comfortably into Orange County's beachside town of Corona del Mar. With their variety of designs, Armet & Davis understood that the roadside suburban restaurant was a new architectural form that required a fresh interpretation of Modernist concepts.

HUDDLE

Within a year of Clock's unveiling, restaurateur Paul S. Cummins entered the Armet & Davis story by commissioning the architects for the aforementioned Restaurant Row location. At an early age, Cummins had worked at a hot dog stand in Cedar Rapids, Iowa. After attending Northwestern University, he launched a successful career in soybean processing and petroleum before starting the Huddle restaurant chain. Set among several fine-dining establishments, this smaller restaurant demanded a sophisticated Modern design in 1952. The existing dinner houses ranged from the Tail o' the Cock's English-country-tavern-themed look to Wayne McAllister's Late Moderne Lawry's Prime Rib. But Los Angeles Modernism was already transitioning in a new direction, represented by the Case Study Houses by Charles Eames, Craig Ellwood, and Raphael Soriano. Whereas Late Moderne emphasized a composition of abstracted planes, shapes, and volumes, newer designs emphasized the direct expression of light, skeletal-exposed structural forms.

Huddle #1, 1954

Armet & Davis's developmental drawings [40-55] track this evolution. Early renderings of Huddle La Cienega show, for example, the integral sign as a vertical dimensional plane—a motif of Late Moderne. The 1954 study above depicts this solid form becoming a lighter, open one: a sign of six poles, each topped by smaller rectangles, one offset from the next, in a jazzier, more weightless design. The later studies have hovering, cantilevered canopies, angled fascias, and diaphanous metal screening on lightweight metal frames, reflecting Armet & Davis's efforts to keep pace with (and at times lead) Modernism innovations.

Cummins became one of the firm's most adventurous clients, approving a series of built and unbuilt custom restaurant designs that furthered their inventive exploration of car-culture Modernism. Armet & Davis remodeled the existing Huddle #1 by adding the Sky Room, a glass observation post reminiscent of an airport control tower—entirely appropriate, as it overlooked the runways of Santa Monica Airport. This was followed by a number of proposals for Cummins that displayed the firm's knack for innovation, formal dexterity, and functionalism. These designs disprove the common criticism that Googie architecture was undisciplined and superficial. Each is worked out conceptually and spatially, integrating inside and out. Each explores the intersection of signage and architecture. Each expresses structure, including Huddle #4's delicate yet bravado forms of thin-shell concrete, also visible in Felix Candela's La Concha Hotel in Puerto Rico, Paul R. Williams's La Concha Motel in Las Vegas, and Eero Saarinen's TWA terminal at JFK Airport; note that Armet & Davis's example came eight years before Saarinen's work at JFK. Armet & Davis would later use prefabricated concrete for the Starlite Club in Gardena, California, in 1960. Though different from the minimalist work of Richard Neutra, each is nonetheless distinctively Modern.

NORM'S

Norm's [pages 68-77] was the next major step as Armet & Davis began to refine the fundamentals of Googie architecture. Studies and presentation drawings in the Norm's archives capture this turning point in design, when partner in charge Eldon Davis worked with his team, including Helen Fong and Lee Linton, to sort through the elements that would come to define Googie. The term Googie was just coming into currency following the publication of *House & Home* editor Douglas Haskell's article "Googie Architecture" in the magazine's February 1952 issue—which focused on John Lautner's 1949 restaurant—though it was not yet an entirely respectable term that an architect would embrace.

That year, 1949, proved to be seminal in Los Angeles architecture. Besides Googies, Lautner's Foster Carling House and Ray and Charles Eames's house were also completed. Wayne McAllister, the dean of drive-in architects, was the mastermind behind Bob's Big Boy on Riverside Drive in Toluca Lake. Combining drive-in service at the rear and counter and table service inside, the iconic restaurant boasted a curving window right out of CinemaScope that looked onto the busy commercial strip before it. To the south, over the Hollywood Hills, Douglas Honnold helmed the design of Tiny Naylor's at Sunset and La Brea. Also a drive-in offering indoor seating, the restaurant's carhop service was sheltered under a long, sweeping canopy that evoked an airplane wing complete with angled struts. Each of these buildings set a standard for using Modern concepts with an experimental vigor responding to function.

Norm's was no different. Former car salesman Norm Roybark opened his namesake restaurant also in 1949 on Sunset. After observing the success of Clock, he hired Armet & Davis to develop designs for a second Norm's, to be built at Figueroa and Manchester. Restaurateurs like Roybark were deeply invested in their businesses. They knew their customers and worked closely with the architects they enlisted. Coffee shops were an altogether new type of restaurant. Positioned somewhere between large dinner houses and old-fashioned greasy spoons, they combined elements of both: reasonable prices, family-friendly food and service, and well-designed contemporary architecture.

Two surviving studies [page 68-71] for Norm's evoke the excitement of invention as Davis and his team began exploring the Modern vocabulary in April 1954. Both schemes are small, compact designs featuring counter and booth seating. Each plays with different roof concepts to give the restaurant a memorable presence on the commercial strip. The sign is another element for study, with auto-scaled three-dimensional "Norm's" signs standing above the rooflines integrating sign into architecture. Linton's easy, free hand reflects an unconstrained attitude toward new ideas.

The ideas investigated in the two earlier schemes led to the innovations in the resulting prototype. We will see more studies like these, demonstrating how Armet & Davis evolved their designs as they addressed the requirements and understood the possibilities of this new, car-oriented architecture. Contrary to a common criticism of the time, their unconventional forms were not "simply for show."

In the final prototype, from August 1955, the roof remains the prominent feature, but it has evolved into a specific structural type: a cantilevered, diamond-shaped truss that tapers upward. The structure shapes the space. At the building's center, over the exhibition kitchen surrounded by counter seating, the ceiling is low. From there it soars upward, creating a panoramic glass wall that allows the space to unite visually with the boulevard outside. The kitchen fixtures on view are custom designed for efficiency and style, the display cases are stainless steel, the walls consist of natural rock and a colorful mix of ceramic tile, the table chairs are by Charles and Ray Eames, and the pendant light fixtures are by George Nelson. The prototypical Modern concepts, materials, spaces, and structures are the same as those seen in the Case Study Houses of the same era. Both Armet & Davis's prototype and Pierre Koenig's Case Study House #22 embody the fundamentals of Modernism equally, but where the latter is intended for a single family, the former is open to all, 24/7.

Norm's design brings together for the first time in Armet & Davis's work the defining elements that we know today as Googie: vivid roof, integrated signage, glassy transparency, and open-plan interior—all using modern materials, concepts, landscaping, design, and all scaled for the automobile.

The Norm's at Figueroa and Manchester became a template for later locations in the chain; each was adjusted according to site, plan, and individual details. Still, it established the future direction for Armet & Davis's work. As the coffee shop concept grew in popularity, Norm's and other chains including Bob's Big Boy, Ships, and Carolina Pines Jr. proliferated. Armet & Davis claimed the largest share of these commissions.

ROMEO'S TIMES SQUARE

The butterfly roof over Romeo's Times Square (1955, page 88) at the prominent corner of Wilshire and Fairfax on the Miracle Mile, confirms that Los Angeles's mid-century commercial designs were as innovative as its residential designs. This roof type was a common Modern motif found on houses by Marcel Breuer, William Krisel, Le Corbusier, Oscar Niemeyer, and others. Armet & Davis set to work adapting it to a commercial purpose. Their success would prove the design's flexibility, but it was a challenge. After all, a residence designed on a human scale was one thing; a public commercial building that had to accommodate both the human scale of the diner inside and the scale of the automobile outside was another.

It turned out that the butterfly roof scaled up perfectly to match the large department stores and office buildings around it. The leading façade, facing Wilshire Boulevard, blended both structure and sign as an integral billboard displaying the name (later changed to Johnie's) in coruscating incandescent and colorful neon light. Though Linton's perspective may seem exaggerated, the actual building matched it, thanks to the asymmetry of the butterfly roof.

Inside, Armet & Davis took advantage of the asymmetric, sloping ceiling to articulate the interior space. Slanting upward at the front, the high ceiling allowed a large artwork mural of Times Square. Descending to a low point at the rear of the restaurant, the ceiling created a more intimate dining area. Its broad cantilever allowed the east facade to be mostly columnless, highlighting the expansive window wall. The architects used this to fashion an elegant turn to the glass corner on Wilshire. Held back from the stone-clad structural pylon, the glass performs solely as a graceful enclosure, erasing the line between indoors and out.

The drawing of the similarly conceived Sierra Inn offers useful comparisons. Undated, it most probably is a later version of Romeo's Times Square, and again illustrates the flexibility of the concept in a larger building. Note the ghost of an even more extensive facade (drawn in reverse on the back of the paper), half again as long, seen at the far left. The larger size allows the glass wall in front to be pushed back, creating a landscaped forecourt with the roof cut away, permitting palms to rise above the roofline.

GOOGIES DOWNTOWN

An eye-catching roofline had become a signature of Googie buildings, presenting Armet & Davis with yet another challenge when they took on the task of the second Googies restaurant, in 1955 [pages 92]. It was on the first floor of the six-story San Carlos Hotel in downtown L.A. The site was a propitious one, located on a corner of Pershing Square across from the prestigious Biltmore Hotel, but it was anomalous for a Googie design: a traditional pedestrian-oriented site, not a wide-open commercial strip. The firm had already finished a small remodel of the original Googies by John Lautner on the Sunset Strip for owner Mort Burton that probably involved enclosing a small rear patio in order to expand the dining room. ("Googie" was a pet name for Burton's wife; little did they both know it would become the moniker for an entire phenomenon of ultramodern roadside architecture.)

Four surviving design studies for the downtown site indicate the care that went into Armet & Davis's designs. The challenges were to work with the existing hotel's structure, to create a transparent frontage connecting inside and outside, and to tie in to Lautner's original design sufficiently to establish the chain's design brand. Davis's hands-on involvement is made clear by one of his handwritten notes: "Dick—do you think this has possibilities? Let's study it out a bit and give Mr. Burton this alternate idea developed some—Davis."

The rust-red color of the roofline and the interior soffit edge is a Googie brand—the first Googies, at Sunset and Crescent Heights, had grabbed attention with its angled roofline of corrugated-metal decking left in the red primer paint color from the factory. Usually used for floor decking, then covered with lightweight concrete, this primer was not intended as a final finish. It was pure California Modernism at work: the shock of a factory-made material used in an unvarnished state to showcase its rugged, raw beauty. Residential Modernists from Bernard Maybeck to William Wurster to Jack Hillmer would leave redwood unpainted to allow its natural beauty to act as ornament, color, and texture, all in one—no need to enhance it with a veneer or carved ornament.

Googies Downtown (Remodel), 1955

One of the studies hews closer to the final Burton-approved design. Playing off Lautner's idea of floating the three-dimensional Googies sign, here it sits on top of the angular roof protruding from the wall of the San Carlos to establish the restaurant's visual and spatial (not to mention stylistic) independence from the old hotel. Glass evaporates the hotel's walls—its structural columns unavoidable but claimed for

Googie with colorful mosaic tile cladding imprinted with the "G" logo. The structure almost disappears. Suburban Modernism holds its own in the center of a traditional downtown.

CAROLINA PINES JR.

Though Southern California long ago became world famous for its Modern residential architecture, Googies coffee shops show that the region's commercial architecture was equally original. Carolina Pines Jr., on La Brea near Sunset [pages 78-87], proves the point. Its form follows the functions of serving a hungry democratic public: it is a vivid landmark seen through the windshield, with a highly effective and original integrated sign and creative indoor/outdoor rooms that take advantage of the local climate and turn the commercial strip into social space. As Modern houses connected residents to the natural environment, Modern commercial buildings connected them to their urban environment without apology. Freed from tradition, the design's complete unity reflects the building's purpose and modern pleasures with forms untethered to historic precedent. The creative expression of structure is seen in the undulating, folded-plate roof and the metal-wire trusses holding shades over the outdoor dining patio. The glass walls maximize the possibilities of modern materials.

Its predecessor, the original Carolina Pines Restaurant, had opened in the mid-1920s on Melrose Avenue. It offered down-home Southern cooking in quaint Southern Colonial-style buildings advertised, in tune with the unthinking racism of the era, using stereotypical caricatures to evoke Southern hospitality. By the 1950s, however, the chain had adopted a more contemporary architecture to keep up with the times.

Carolina Pines Jr. demonstrates how the Googie aesthetic expanded Modernism. Hardly minimalist in the International Style mode, it is rich with varied colors, forms, and textures. Such designs indicate that Googie was not simply flashy gimmicks but carefully composed spatial and formal concepts that modulated between the larger public realm and the more intimate human dining space.

As Carolina Pines Jr. expanded to other locations (built and unbuilt), Armet & Davis began to fashion a recognizable brand for the chain. Though these were custom designs, the rendering of an unbuilt Carolina Pines Jr. in Fullerton (1956,

page 82) shows an effort to use the folded-plate roof and hourglass sign to create an instantly recognizable image. Carolina Pines #2 (1961, pages 82-83), on Vermont Avenue, was initially envisioned with the distinctive motifs of the sine-wave roof and the hourglass sign but evolved into a different expression: a scalloped folded-plate roof and a sensuous sculptural sign grounding the building to the earth. By this point, Lee Linton had left the firm. Without his trademark hand, the graphic style of the Vermont drawings grows softer, though still sophisticated.

The Carolina Pines Jr. location in Encino (1965, page 87), on Ventura Boulevard's prime commercial strip, reflects the transition of Armet & Davis's concepts to a new phase in the 1960s. The motif of natural stone pylons and terrace walls rising from the ground (as seen at Romeo's Times Square, today Johnie's, since 1955) now holds aloft the carapace roof introduced at Pann's (1956), wherein the geometric striping of colored rock reinforces the roof's profile and its visual impact. (Though Pann's survives today as one of Los Angeles's best-known examples of Googie, its original drawings have not been located.) The rendering of the Encino restaurant is done in watercolor in a realistic, less expressionistic manner, and conveys less of the character of the architecture than Linton's energized drawings do.

DENNY'S

As the restaurant industry shifted in the late 1950s and 1960s toward burgeoning chains, Armet & Davis found themselves creating prototype designs that could be built anywhere. Having established a visual brand, they were able to control building and operational costs. Clients across the country included Eppie's, White Spot, Roy Rogers, Preb's, the Bob's Big Boy franchisees, and especially Denny's [pages 114-118].

Where Armet & Davis's custom designs such as those for Romeo's Times Square and Wich Stand experimented with formal and spatial possibilities, their prototype designs amplified the Googie essentials: a dramatically engineered roof balanced on natural stone pillars, a sign blended with the design, and a broad, glassy frontage. Denny's (1957; originally Danny's before the popular chain Coffee Dan's threatened to sue) distilled these elements into a brand built coast to coast.

The initial prototype [page 116] is one of Armet & Davis's numerous extant designs, and perhaps the most prolific. Outside, the boomerang-shaped roof is impossible to miss; inside, it creates a dramatic, high-ceilinged space, the very opposite of a minimalist box in the image of Mies van der Rohe's Modernism. The roof rests on a natural stone pylon tapering up from a wide base buried in the earth to a precise balance point for the boomerang roof. The implied energy in that pivot point, the off-kilter angles, and the singular vertical accent of the sign piercing the roof create a dynamic composition typical of Googie design.

By 1966, Harold Butler, founder of Denny's, wanted a new prototype. Once again, Googie architecture became the cultural bellwether that tapped into the changing times. The roof of the second prototype remained prominently visible to motorists and still highlighted its dogleg beams, but its newly introduced, tall, central shingled section gave it the flavor of a jazzy mansard roof—a traditional architecture style soon to come back into fashion.

BOB'S BIG BOY

Throughout the 1950s, Bob Wian of Bob's Big Boy continued to work with Wayne McAllister, McAllister's partner William Wagner, and architect S. David Underwood to realize custom buildings and a prototype. In 1958, however, he turned to Armet & Davis to develop a second prototype. As Wian franchised his restaurants regionally, Armet & Davis found their business increasing nationwide for Wian and for Big Boy franchisees Azar's, Frisch's, Manners, and Elias Bros. [pages 126–149]. Because sites varied region by region, Armet & Davis could experiment with a multitude of different structures.

After Wian sold the business to the Marriott Corporation in 1967, Marriott commissioned the firm for yet another prototype, in 1974. Ironically, by then Modernism in general had come to look old-fashioned. Society's enthusiasm over futuristic technology had cooled, and Postmodernism began reacquainting architects with historic styles. Reflecting this cultural trend, Armet & Davis developed a gabled, Ranch-house style prototype building in a less bold, more residentially scaled design that incorporated more wood than metal.

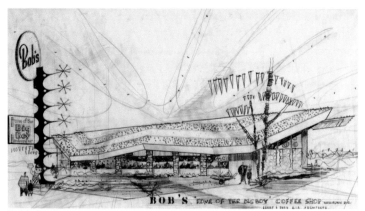

Bob's Big Boy, c. 1957

SMALLER SELF-SERVICE RESTAURANTS

Googie architecture was more than a set of wild, eye-catching shapes pasted onto ordinary buildings. Dinner houses were one thing, coffee shops were another, and coffee shops with drive-in service were yet another, followed by filling stations, car dealerships, bowling alleys, car washes, and motels. Each expressed a distinct aspect of modern life that drew its form and plan from its function.

This dimension of Googie becomes clear when we look at Armet & Davis's small walk-up or drive-through stands that needed to address different demands than those of their full-size siblings. We can study this in a series of alternative designs for Marriott Corporation's Hot Shoppes chain. In direct competition with McDonald's (whose golden-arched prototype buildings, conceived by architect Stanley Meston, were quickly spreading across the country) and Jack in the Box (whose whimsical, toylike prototype was the work of architects Smith and Williams), Marriott realized the value of an appealing architectural image as a selling point.

These designs had to turn a small structure into an imposing landmark on the commercial strip. The collection is a course in taking a few simple elements—height, an exposed structure, a roof enclosure with sufficient character to lead the eye, a freestanding sign that reinterprets the structure's motif, and natural materials—and combining them inventively to create roadside drama.

Armet & Davis designed other self-service restaurants throughout the 1950s and 1960s. McCarthy's [page 61] is a full-fledged example of early Googie, with its extruded L-shaped roof dominating the small stand beneath it. Taco Sombrero [page 194] riffs on the ever-popular Brown Derby— the grandfather of roadside restaurants that has come to occupy a larger, totemistic place in popular memory.

The Chicken Fry [page 162] embraces theme architecture through its A-frame embellished with carved beam ends, tikis, torches, tapas cloth ornament, and tropical landscaping. The impact of Jack in the Box's drive-through service is seen in the concept for the By The Number Self Service Restaurant (1963, page 189). These designs continued to draw from a range of evocative geometries such as the triangulated fascia of the White Spot in Denver (1963, page 188).

OTHER BUILDING TYPES

Googie served the car-culture city very well. Car washes, car dealerships, bowling alleys, motels, country clubs, and shopping centers were all part of the lifestyle of suburban mid-century America, In turn, Armet & Davis's architectural designs were part of a larger urban design strategy that organized the commercial streetscapes of the new suburban metropolises.

Bowling alleys, like coffee shops, were often the first public buildings to take form in the new suburbs of the post-war period, serving social as well as commercial purposes. No client knew that better than Marlow-Burns. One of the chief builders of the era, this company fashioned master-planned communities that combined housing, shopping, recreation, and parks. Westchester was built for defense workers in the run-up to World War II, followed by Panorama City during the post-war boom. El Rodeo Bowl's design [page 66] was clearly conceived as a civic landmark and social center as well as a recreation venue. The enormous sign, featuring a bowling pin and bowling ball, though never built, reaffirmed Googie's roots in the programmatic architecture of Los Angeles from the 1920s on, with its giant derbies, oranges, shoes, and flowerpots meant to establish the landmark status of a building.

The Holiday Bowl [page 120] is another example of the social community that Googie buildings provided. Located in South Central L.A., it was a gathering place where members of the Japanese American community came to participate in

bowling leagues. This provided the communal activity, while the coffee shop and lounge provided the social space. In designing the lounge interior, Helen Fong placed cork panels on the ceiling to form a map of the Japanese archipelago lined in gold foil, a nod to the Holiday Bowl's frequent occupants.

Armet & Davis worked on casinos as well, from the Starlite Club in Gardena, California, to the showroom of the Riviera Hotel [page 155] on the country's ultimate commercial zone, the Las Vegas Strip. The Starlite Club [page 168–171] boasted a daring structure of thin-shell concrete, another expressive modern building technology. The new technique, pioneered by the Mexican architect-engineer Felix Candela and Spanish architect Eduardo Torroja, used repetitive sculptural modules. Armet & Davis adapted a similar structure for the Main Street Shopping Center.

The firm's vision for its Googie Modern motels paired well with that of its coffee shops. The Carolina-Hollywood Motel [page 86] adjacent to the Carolina Pines Jr. Coffee Shop on La Brea is one such example. In another, the wings of a two-story motel wrapped around a Denny's restaurant as its centerpiece; these creations appeared in Auburn, Reno, and Palm Springs. An unbuilt Bob's Big Boy was to be part of a five-story motor hotel featuring a novel spiral auto ramp that would enable lodgers to drive directly to their rooms.

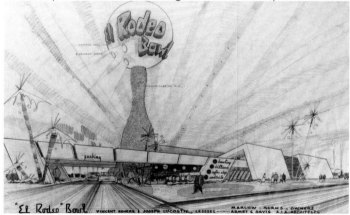

El Rodeo Bowl, c. 1955

In projects like the aforementioned and the Palm Springs Sands Hotel, Armet & Davis developed Googie Modern's potential to organize groupings of roadside buildings into larger and larger complexes. The architects followed an aesthetic and urban planning theory that contrasted with prevailing academic concepts. While notable planners and critics such as Lewis Mumford, Catherine Bauer Wurster, Victor Gruen, Peter Blake, and Mary Mix Foley were decrying the "slopopolis," "vulgarity," "raucous ugliness," and even "kitsch" of the commercial strip (and winning the hearts of many city planners and tastemakers), other planners and academics saw value. For these observers, pragmatism, creative vigor, color, form, and responsiveness to popular life and interests offered feasible alternatives. The commercial strip was not to be erased; its lessons on organizing cities, responding to modern technology, and listening to popular taste were to be learned, refined, and applied. Lloyd Wright had recognized this early in the evolution of Googie through his work on Los Angeles's Yucca-Vine Market (1928). This group of observers included J.B. Jackson, Tom Wolfe, Douglas Haskell, Robert Venturi, Denise Scott Brown, and Steven Izenour, who, in spite of howls of rage from high art circles, championed the roadside vernacular, especially as realized on the Las Vegas Strip.

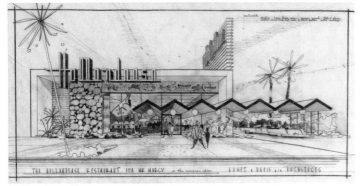

Hollandease Restaurant, 1952–1953

Though they received little critical attention in the 1950s and 1960s, Armet & Davis were part of this latter group—except that they were building, not just theorizing. In the very real world of the restaurant industry, city planning, and commercial design, this commercial architecture firm was designing and erecting scores of buildings that became part of the daily lives of millions of North Americans. They drew on and built for segments of society that were not usually considered a respectable or notable part of the culture. As families began decamping to the suburbs, Armet & Davis welcomed them with a newly devised landscape. When teenagers cruised commercial strips in their hot rods and stock cars, they stopped to enjoy a burger at Stanley Burke's or Bob's Big Boy on Van Nuys Boulevard. Far from being teenagers, Louis Armet and Eldon Davis had sophisticated architectural educations and

were well versed in the Organic architectural tradition of Frank Lloyd Wright. But they also learned from restaurateurs Norm Roybark, Paul S. Cummins, Harold Butler, Mort Burton, and Matthew Shipman. Furthermore, they lived and worked in Los Angeles, where these new architectural concepts were commonplace and accepted, even encouraged.

A unified aesthetic landscape was blooming in this environment. It could be witnessed from dashboard to coffee shop counter, from the coolest customized car to the family's Chevy station wagon as each pulled into the parking lot of a Bob's Big Boy. Ever alert to such shifts, Wolfe reported on this emerging pan-cultural movement rooted in growing Los Angeles.

Call it Kustom Kulture, a phrase that was common then and useful today. It encompassed new, recreational phenomena like surfing and skateboarding, and aesthetic phenomena like surf music, pinstriping, and decals. Designers including Von Dutch, Ed "Big Daddy" Roth, and George Barris made a name for themselves through their work and well-crafted countercultural personas as they toiled in their out-of-the-way garage studios in South Gate, Lynwood, and the San Fernando Valley. Indeed, the cars that are prominently incorporated into many Armet & Davis drawings are usually not identifiable as a particular make, yet they are carefully conceived to evoke the zoom, flash, and sophistication of the times. The cars go with the architecture and the architecture goes with the cars, so clearly that the connection is obvious. Cars and buildings—and people—were all part of a unified aesthetic landscape.

Kustom Kulture, in its full impact, moved beyond these flamboyant personalities into the heart of American industry. Charles Jordan, director of design (and later vice president in charge of design) for Cadillac at General Motors, kept close tabs on custom car design in Southern California because it was a sensitive barometer of social trends, as Tom Wolfe wrote. Likewise, Louis Armet and Eldon Davis were, in demeanor, straightforward professional commercial architects delivering a reliable product to hard-nosed restaurateurs. Yet Googie was an indispensable part of the emerging Kustom Kulture that was shaping so much of California—and American—cities and lifestyles during the mid-century building boom.

Falcon, 1956

Googie and Kustom Kulture surveyed the vibrant, pragmatic, and at times glorious architecture of the suburban commercial strip. Mining vernacular cultures has always led to the mother lode whenever creative figures recognized it. They heeded its rules and understood its insights into how people wanted to live. They observed the strip's broad horizontal landscape and acted on its potential, punctuating it with signs and rooflines that would help orient motorists driving through its random clutter of telephone poles, stoplights, and scattered businesses. Other creatives—Victor Gruen, for one—had observed the same landscape, saw little to recommend it, and decided to replace it with an entirely new urban form, the shopping mall. Most observers at the time viewed these as two opposed approaches and took sides as to which should prevail. Today we can determine that both are legitimate alternatives, that they existed and thrived side by side, and that they have lessons to teach us, if we take the time to look.

That is the aim of this book. Through the original vision of Armet & Davis's architecture presented in the pages that follow, Googie remains a central part of the fertile architectural and planning environment of Southern California in this era. Well-known high-art architects and critics rarely acknowledged Googie Modern, but it is not a superficial gloss. Rather, it is an effective response to the trends that run deep in culture, in technology, and in life.

PORTFOLIO:
ARMET DAVIS NEWLOVE
/ 1947–1974

ARMET & DAVIS A.I.A. ARCHITECTS
2440 WEST THIRD STREET
LOS ANGELES 57, CALIFORNIA

Though critics and historians paid little attention to Armet & Davis in the 1950s and 1960s, the significance of the firm's work has since become clear. Armet Davis Newlove (ADN) buildings are being landmarked and restored some sixty years after they were built.

Many architects have worked under the burden of knowing (or presuming) that they were making major contributions to the history of architecture, and so made conscious efforts to preserve their drawings. Sometimes they erased evidence of projects they did not want shared with the public. Armet & Davis did not labor under that burden. They were commercial architects focused on serving their clients, not on designing for the history books. They kept a complete and accessible archive only because it proved useful when clients returned—as they often did—for additions, remodels, or a new building. Nonetheless, today the archive is an enormous boon to scholarship and preservation. The drawings that the office has protected, under partner Victor Newlove's watch, are a treasure trove of mid-century design unlike any other.

The drawings are presented in roughly chronological order; however, the drawings for certain major clients produced over the span of many years (Huddle, Carolina Pines, Googies, Norm's, Denny's, Bob's Big Boy, Hot Shoppes) are grouped together so they can be more easily studied. The work includes large-scale (3 by 4 feet) presentation drawings, informal design development studies, and photographic reproductions of presentation drawings for advertising, promotion, and portfolios, often with added color in pencil, Magic Marker, watercolor, or other media. Black-and-white pencil drawings occasionally have colored pencil or other media applied directly to the original. We have included information on dates, locations, illustrator, and client, in addition to whether a building was completed and its current condition, when that information could be confirmed.

The portfolio includes most of ADN's key designs, though drawings of key projects such as Pann's, Ships La Cienega, Tiny Naylor's La Cienega, and Laurel Canyon Carwash could not be located. It is our hope that a thorough cataloging by an institutional archive will uncover more of this invaluable collection of California Modernism, and especially, what we call Googie Modern.

In these pages, occasional photo collages show selected drawings superimposed on their original sites, as built or as intended. The contrast between the original Armet & Davis designs and the current commercial architecture that has replaced them demonstrates the decline of architectural quality in our present-day landscape.

CLOCK #11
Los Angeles, CA, 1951

Armet & Davis's first coffee shop design for this then very well-established restaurant demonstrates how the necessity of communicating a building's purpose in the car-culture landscape required a bold scale and a modern geometry.
| Built; demolished

6819 La Tijera Blvd., Los Angeles

THE HOLLANDEASE RESTAURANT FOR MR. MARCY *in the mondrian*

HOLLANDEASE RESTAURANT
Bellflower, California, 1952–1953

materials
plaster · large flake mica · ceramic mural · tinted glass ·
washed round river bed rock in black mortar · metal canopy ··

ARMET & DAVIS a.i.a ARCHITECTS

"In the mondrian [sic] idiom," Linton notes on the title block, showing the breadth of the Armet & Davis office. The architects took the rectilinear aesthetic of Bauhaus Modernism and enriched it with the varied textures, mosaic tile murals, and signage of the Googie aesthetic. The sign is the facade, the facade is the sign, in three-dimensional lettering. Various materials, listed in the upper right corner, include plaster, large flake mica, ceramic mural, tinted glass, washed round river bed rock in black mortar, metal canopy. All are integrated in the offices' trademark ways: the rounded rocks in black mortar, the inset louvered wall as a backdrop to planting, the brightly colored ceramic tile band mural over the entry, and, of course, the window wall that puts the well-illuminated interior on full display.

Linton seemed to favor aquatic figures—see Carolina Pines Jr. [page 80]. The drawing conveys a sense of dimensional depth, drawing the viewer into a restaurant populated by stylish women and men. 5,200-square-foot, 150-person capacity restaurant with a budget of $125,000 in 1953.
| Client: Mr. Marcy | Rendering by Lee Linton | Built; demolished

HUDDLE RESTAURANTS

1952–1955

HUDDLE #2 LA CIENEGA (STUDY)
Beverly Hills, California, 1952-1953

Armet & Davis did many studies for various Huddle locations [pages 40-54], demonstrating their flexibility manipulating the vocabulary, scale, and functional expressions of Googie Modern architecture. Huddle #1 was a remodel; Huddle #2 was the first entirely new structure designed for the chain. This initial design was for a building larger than the final site allowed. It included a porte cochere, at left.
| Client: Paul S. Cummins | Rendering by Lee Linton | Built; altered

HUDDLE #2 LA CIENEGA (STUDY)
Beverly Hills, California, 1952–1953

Client: Paul S. Cummins | Rendered by Lee Linton | Built & Altered

RESTAURANT

TECTS   4-15-53

163 N. La Cienega Blvd., Beverly Hills

This early study for Huddle #2, at left, represents the size of the final design. It shows the integral sign as a vertical dimensional plane—a motif of Late Moderne. The previous spread shows how this solid form became lighter and more open: a sign of six poles, each topped by a smaller rectangle, one offset from the next—a jazzier, weightless design. Both versions feature hovering cantilevered canopies, angled fascias, and transparent walls of glass.
| Client: Paul S. Cummins | Rendering by Lee Linton | Built; altered

HUDDLE #1
3030 S. BUNDY LOS ANGELES
ARMET & DAVIS

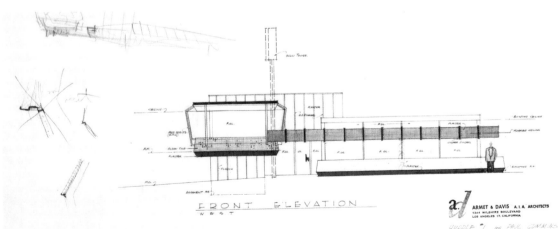

FRONT ELEVATION
WEST

ad ARMET & DAVIS A.I.A. ARCHITECTS
1244 WILSHIRE BOULEVARD
LOS ANGELES 17, CALIFORNIA

HUDDLE #1 on PAUL CUMMINS

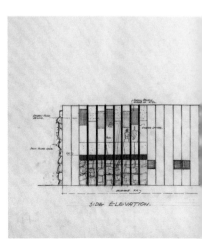

SIDE ELEVATION.

HUDDLE #1
Los Angeles, 1954

In Lee Linton's color drawing at left, top, the faceted glass lounge sits like a gem in an angular setting of colorful mosaic tiles. Its angled, rather than strict, rectilinear forms explore the varied geometries of Organic design, also seen in Los Angeles in the work of A. Quincy Jones, John Lautner, and Whitney Smith. Bottom left: two hard-lined elevation drawings show another step in the design process—beyond the atmospheric presentation drawings—with refined details, dimensions, and materials.

| Built; demolished

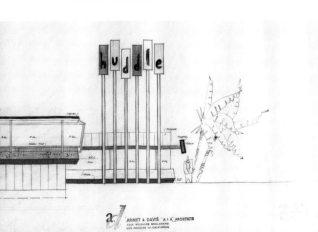

3010 S. Bundy Dr., Los Angeles

HUDDLE #4 RESTAURANT for MR. PAUL CUMMINS
armet & davis, aia, architects

HUDDLE RESTAURANT #4 (VARIOUS STUDIES)
Pasadena, California, 1954

The design for Huddle #4, at left, went through several iterations, including this A-frame version similar to Palmer and Krisel's later Coffee Dan's (1957) on Van Nuys Boulevard. This unbuilt design, however, pulls the A-frame in two, using glass to fill the gap. Delicately framed art-glass panels embedded with circles of colored glass ornament the end wall. Above, an interior view shows how a high-ceilinged space can be differentiated with Modern chandeliers, soffits, decorative screens, and walls. The exhibition cooking feature is at left.

| Client: Paul S. Cummins | Renderings by Lee Linton

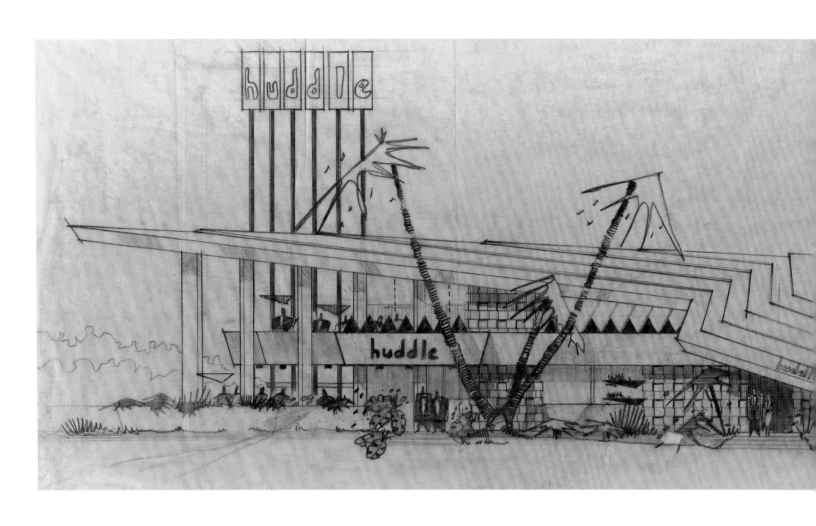

Two variations on a two-story restaurant use bold, A-frame, carapace-like roofs. In one version, shown at right, the roof touches the ground. Each shows the careful integration of outdoor roof terraces, mezzanines overlooking dining rooms, asymmetrical rooflines, walls of patterned concrete block, Organic fenestration designs, secondary entries, and standing-seam roofs, all under a unified form.
| Client: Paul S. Cummins | Rendering by Lee Linton

JAN. 27 54

FREE STANDING SIGN TOWER

#4

HUDDLE RESTAURANT (PROPOSALS)
Pasadena, California, 1954

The most robust study for this restaurant, depicted in the drawing at right, was planned with a vaulted, thin concrete shell structure over a two-level restaurant, similar to the Modern structures of architects Felix Candela and Paul R. Williams. In the rendering below, Googie's bold forms turn the entire building into a sign to attract motorists' attention on the commercial strip. Boasting diaphanous screens, mosaics, glass walls, pendant light fixtures, and landscaping, the total composition is far from minimalist but unmistakably Modern.
| Client: Paul S. Cummins | Renderings by Lee Linton

Huddle ♯ 4 in Pasadena
FOR MR. PAUL CUMMINS.   ARMET & DAVIS A.I.A. ARCHITECTS.

LEE LINTON - ARCHITECT
S & MR. LOU LESSER ....

HUDDLE RESTAURANT #3
West Covina, California, 1955

One facade, at left in the drawing, features a series of the letter "h" in four large-scale figures, each on its own flap. Each "h" is covered in mesh and lit from the rear, emitting a glow at night. Behind the flaps are perforated metal panels alternating with naturalistic

FlagCrete masonry (artificial stone). This mix of natural and manufactured textures, structure, signage, and landscaping demonstrates Googie Modern design's flexibility and ability to show the beauty in modern manufactured materials.
| Client: Paul S. Cummins | Rendering by Lee Linton

Huddle #3

HUDDLE RESTAURANT #3 (INTERIOR STUDIES)
West Covina, California, 1955

HUDDLE #3 RESTAURANT

ARMET & DAVIS AIA ARCHITECTS
23 MAY 1955

These interior colors are not the primary reds, yellows, and blues used by many European Modernists who were influenced by Mondrian; rather, they make up a soft, earthy palette—dusty roses, mustard yellows, and sage greens blend with natural plants. Artwork panels and screens of abstract shapes and textures were often fabricated of plastic, a modern technology recognized for its artistic possibilities. Huddle was a full-service restaurant with a bar and lounge, but Armet & Davis coffee shops frequently used similar custom artwork designed by artists and craftspeople including Hans Werner, Betsy Hancock, Roger Darricarrere, Fred Glassman, and Bijan Shokatfard.
| Client: Paul S. Cummins | Rendering by Lee Linton

MARCY'S
c. 1953

This early design helps to document the evolving character of Armet & Davis and the firm's search for new architectural solutions. The rectangular pylon sign with the name Marcy's Coffee Shop splashed across it shows the influence of existing models such as Wayne McAllister's Bob's Big Boy in Toluca Lake. The intriguing, exposed post-and-beam structure along the front reflects Davis and Armet's studies at the USC School of Architecture, where they learned about the style from architect and instructor Calvin Straub. Innovative sunscreens that can be lowered into place show the partners exploring ingenious new directions for coffee shop architecture and enlivening the facade. Note that the drawing calls out "Panels made of several textured materials, painted bright colors[;] each can be lowered for West sun."

| Client: Charles Marcy

ROBERT HILL'S CHEFS INN
Corona del Mar, California, 1954

As Armet & Davis launched into coffee shop design, they also worked on a number of upscale restaurants and dinner houses such as this one. A low-slung gabled roof, ending in a landscaped outdoor dining patio, seen at right in the sketch above, is sheltered by a decorative fence that reflects elements of the Southern California Ranch house. Note the antenna-like fixture rising from the roof. At left, the roadside sign is a sophisticated design with sign boxes cantilevered out from a stone pylon, alternating on each side to introduce depth and shadow. It ties in with the main building via a porte cochere, and the sign's stone is repeated in the chimney at the building's opposite end.
| Rendering by Lee Linton | Built; demolished

YANKEE DOODLE DRIVE-IN
1954

As they were inventing the look of the California coffee shop, Armet & Davis designed a range of food service types. This one is a combination coffee shop and drive-in; note the covered canopies for car service, at right. The design of the waitresses' uniforms was coordinated with the architecture. Conceived around the time of Norm's, the restaurant incorporates Googie elements: FlagCrete masonry on the columns and base of the building, steel columns with a lightened web support for the canopies, and landscaping integrated into the structure through holes in the eave. Note the ovoid hanging lamps inside by George Nelson, which were often used by Armet & Davis along with Eames chairs, underscoring the shared aesthetic of so-called popular and high-art architecture.

| Client: W. P. Bigelow | Rendering by Lee Linton | Built; demolished

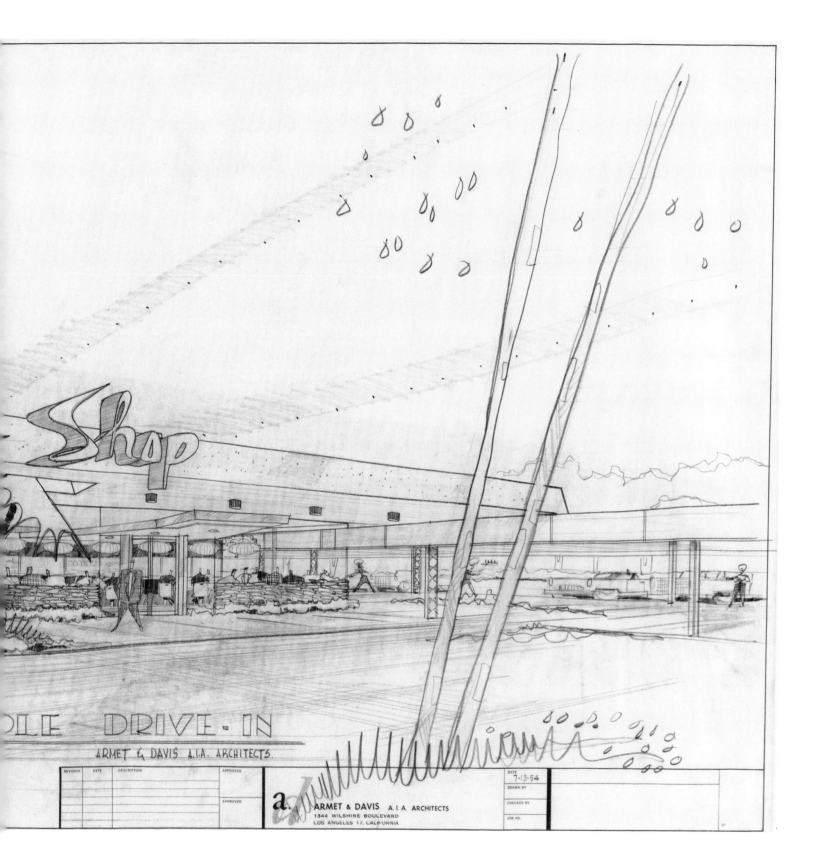

Shop

OLE - DRIVE - IN

ARMET & DAVIS A.I.A. ARCHITECTS.

REVISION	DATE	DESCRIPTION	APPROVED			DATE 7-13-54	
						DRAWN BY	
			APPROVED	**a.** ARMET & DAVIS A.I.A. ARCHITECTS		CHECKED BY	
				1344 WILSHIRE BOULEVARD LOS ANGELES 17, CALIFORNIA		JOB NO.	

BACKLITED SIGN BOARD
REARRANGEABLE LETTERS
(THEATRE MARQUIS TYPE)

McCARTHY'S   SELF-

VICE RESTAURANT

ET & DAVIS, A.I.A., ARCHITECTS
ANGELES,   CALIF.

McCARTHY'S SELF-SERVICE RESTAURANT
c. 1954

Though undated, this drawing appears to be from around
1954. It is a walk-up stand designed to compete with
contemporary fast-food stands such as McDonald's and
Jack in the Box. The roof and the sign are unified, as in later
Armet & Davis designs, and trees are made an integral part
of the design through openings in the roof. The architects
emphasize the perspective by placing the viewpoint near
the ground.
| Rendering by Lee Linton

COFFEE SHOP for MR. LOUIS LESSER & MR. RUSSELL ALOTIS.
ARMET & DAVIS AIA ARCHITECTS

chef's hat COFFEE SHOP FOR RUSSELL ALOTIS, LESSEE   LOUIS LESSER, OWNER
ARMET & DAVIS, ARCHITECTS

CHEF'S HAT COFFEE SHOP
Los Angeles, 1954

Restaurant names on these designs were sometimes placeholders to give a client an idea of the concept. This elegant gull-wing roof performs two functions: first, as seen from the road, it has a strong, clean form; second, the roof's spatial performance leads patrons in as it slopes down into the center of the building and the long counter facing the exhibition kitchen—the show, the entertainment. The spaces at each end are enclosed on three sides by glass, creating a garden room. Note how the sign echoes the V-shaped roof.
| Owner: Louis Lesser | Client: Russell Alotis | Rendering by Lee Linton

Ron·dee COFFEE SHOP   SAN FERNANDO , CALIFORNIA

for mr. floyd j. bulrice & mr. neil nutzmann

ARMET & DAVIS, A.I.A. ARCHITECTS

RON-DEE COFFEE SHOP
Sylmar, California, 1955

The pronounced asymmetry of Ron-Dee's hovering folded roof over irregular zigzagging walls was an especially advanced design concept in 1955. In the built version, this was emphasized by the tilt of the open-web girder piercing through the roof and supporting a three-sided sign anchored by guy wires. The "3-D" billboard created by the glass walls showing off the interior is evident in the color rendering above.
| Client: Floyd J. Bulrice and Neil Nutzmann | Rendering by Lee Linton | Built; demolished

12341 San Fernando Rd., Sylmar

Stan's DRIVE-IN ADDITION
HIGHLAND & SUNSET BOULEVARDS   ARMET

STAN'S DRIVE-IN, ADDITION
Los Angeles, CA, c. 1955

The circular portion of the building on the left was an original Simon's drive-in restaurant by Wayne McAllister. Afte Stanley Burke bought the chain in 1950, he asked Armet & Davis to add on a dining room—an interesting transition from the classic 1930s drive-in to the 1950s coffee shop.

| Client: Stanley Burke | Rendering by Lee Linton | Not built

ROTATING BALL

3 COLORED SPOTS

SCINTILLATING "PIN"

parking

"El Rodeo" Bowl   VINCENT REHERS & JOSEPH LUCOSTIC, LESS

MARLOW - BURNS , OWNERS
.... ARMET & DAVIS A.I.A. ARCHITECTS

EL RODEO BOWL
Los Angeles, c. 1955

In the rapidly developing suburbs of the 1950s, bowling alleys served as community centers, recreational venues, friendly watering holes with cocktail lounges and coffee shops, and meeting rooms for Boy Scouts, Girl Scouts, sewing clubs, and any sundry social entity that needed a space in which to gather. This design speaks of the bowling alley's role as a civic and social landmark in the new car-culture landscape. Though not built, the pin would have been covered in scintillating incandescent bulbs, the bowling ball on top would have rotated, and colored spotlights would have shot from its three finger holes—unmistakable landmarks of the growing suburban metropolis. The owners, Marlow-Burns, were one of Southern California's primary developers of master-planned suburbs, including Panorama City and Westchester. | Owner: Marlow-Burns | Client: Vincent Rehers and Joseph Lucostic | Rendering by Lee Linton | Built; altered

NORM'S RESTAURANTS
1954–1956

NORM'S, SCHEME "B"
Los Angeles, 1954

Two surviving studies for one of Armet & Davis's most influential designs, shown here and on the following spread, confirm how carefully the architects studied architectural and site-planning features. The scale and visibility of the roof, the placement of the signage, and the interior configuration were thoroughly investigated and then integrated into a unified design, belying criticism of Googie as shallow sensationalism intended only to grab attention.

Scheme "B" is a strikingly open, light composition, featuring a porte cochere (de rigueur at fancy dinner houses on La Cienega's Restaurant Row) that leads customers to a small, glass-enclosed waiting room with counter seating and booths beyond. The roofline is the major feature: a large arch rising high into the air, functioning to attract attention and connect to the public's burgeoning interest in modern living. | Client: Norman Roybark | Rendering by Lee Linton

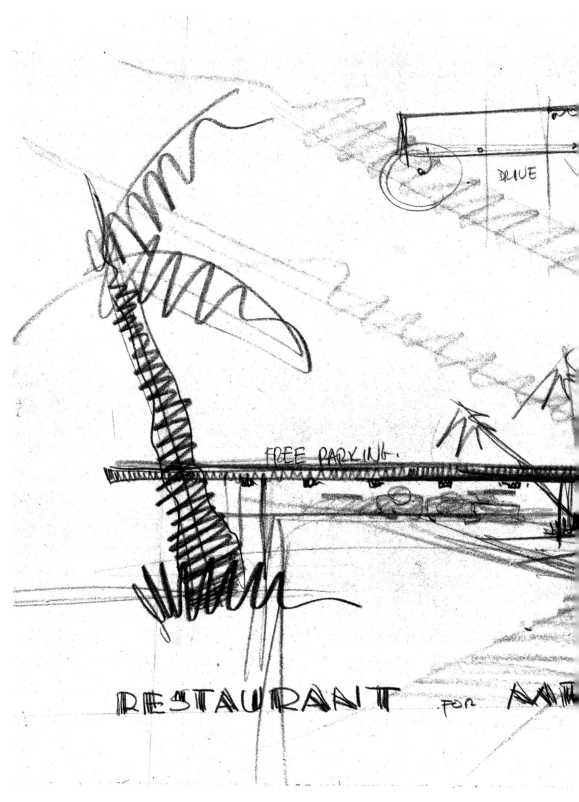

FREE PARKING.

DRIVE

RESTAURANT FOR AN

NORM'S, SCHEME "C"
Los Angeles, 1954

Scheme "C" features an upswept, splayed A-frame roof over a different plan from that of Scheme "B." Here, a freestanding "Norm's" sign rides the ridge line. The structure determines the interior plan, creating high, wide, and airy spaces at the front, sloping down to draw the eye to the counter seating around the central exhibition kitchen, and ending in a flat roof at the rear of the building.
| Client: Norman Roybark
| Rendering by Lee Linton

SERVICE

BOOTHS.

OUTER

NORM'S

NORMAN ROYBARK

ARMET & DAVIS A.I.A. ARCHITECTS SCHEME "C" 4-23-54

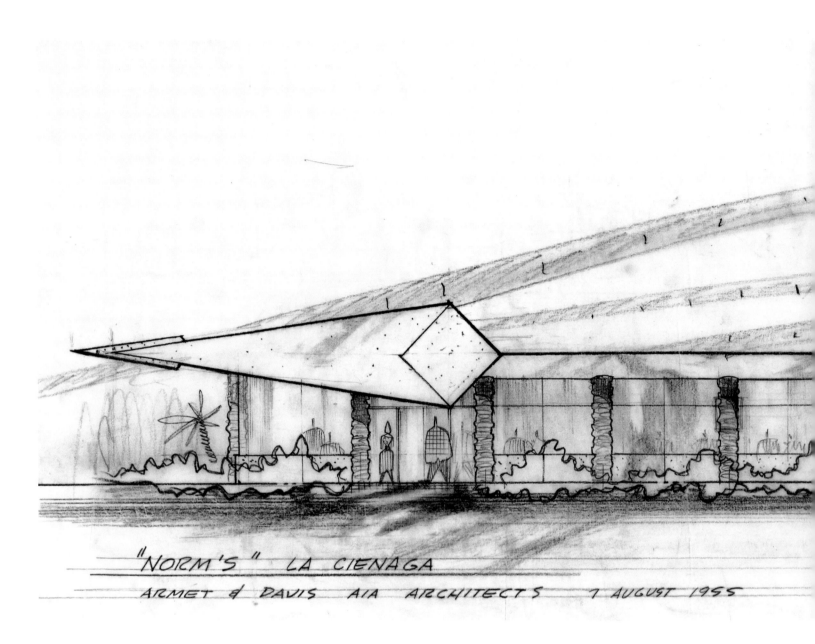

"NORM'S" LA CIENAGA

ARMET & DAVIS AIA ARCHITECTS   7 AUGUST 1955

NORM'S #4 LA CIENEGA (PROTOTYPE)
Los Angeles, 1955

The result of the studies on the previous pages was this prototype, built first at Figueroa Street and Manchester Avenue in 1954, and then on La Cienega Boulevard in 1955. The cantilevered, diamond-shaped roof truss diminishes in thickness and weight, creating even larger expanses of glass that open the main dining area to the view of bustling Figueroa. Helen Fong's sensitivity to human-scale details creates a more intimate space, with U-shaped banquette booths at the rear (at right) screened off by original artwork consisting of free-form plastic elements. The building was declared a Los Angeles Historical-Cultural Monument in 2015.
| Client: Norman Roybark | Rendering by Lee Linton | Built; extant

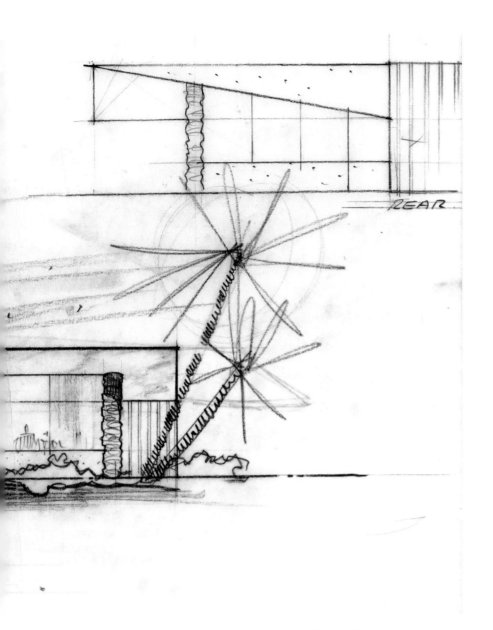

REAR

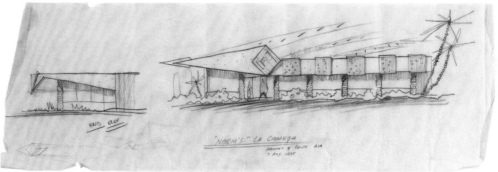

END ELEV

"NORM'S" LA CIENEGA
ARMÉT & DAVIS AIA
7 NOV. 1955

"NORM'S" LA CIENAGA

ARMET & DAVIS AIA ARCHITECTS   7 AUG.

REAR

1955

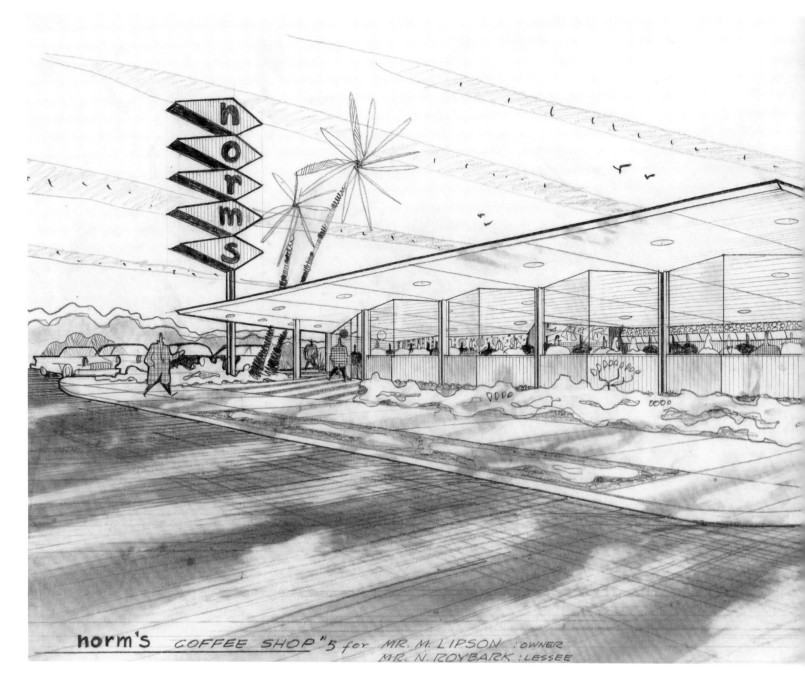

norm's COFFEE SHOP #5 for MR. M. LIPSON :OWNER
MR. N. ROYBARK :LESSEE

NORM'S COFFEE SHOP #5
Culver City, California, 1956

An unbuilt variation of the pennant-shaped Norm's roof appears above. This rendering shows the sign's final design by Eldon Davis, still used by Norm's. The neon pennants spelling out the restaurant's name echo the roof's shape, integrating the sign into the architecture. Animated neon, which illuminates the letters and, in turn, the background, is also part of the design. Each aspect of Googie architecture needed to be as effective by night as it was by day. "Helen wanted the sign to dance," recalls Victor Newlove.
| Owner: M. Lipson | Lessee: Norman Roybark | Rendering by Lee Linton

ARMET & DAVIS, AIA, ARCHITECTS

1·20·56

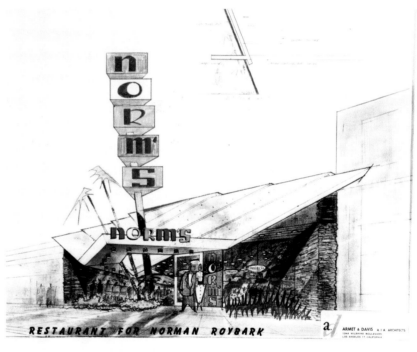

RESTAURANT FOR NORMAN ROYBARK

ARMET & DAVIS A I A ARCHITECTS
1344 WILSHIRE BOULEVARD
LOS ANGELES 17 CALIFORNIA

NORM'S
Los Angeles, c. 1956

Armet & Davis designed an alternative for a mid-block restaurant in which the roof was still dominant, as indicated in the color drawing above. Like a piece of origami, the A-frame form tilts up at the entry, creating a void in the roof that allows palm trees and the integrated sign to jut through. This same roof structure continues inside over the counter, uniting inside and out and drawing the eye into the space.

| Client: Norman Roybark | Rendering by Lee Linton

CAROLINA PINES JR. RESTAURANTS

1954–1955

CAROLINA PINES JR. COFFEE SHOP
Los Angeles, 1955

The Carolina Pines Jr. chain was another important Armet & Davis client. The design shown at right integrates both auto and human scale on busy La Brea Avenue. At left in the drawing, an outdoor seating area under the light, angled steel trusses is topped by hanging canvas shades, while the enormous hourglass-shaped signboard looms behind to catch the eye of motorists. The lettering spills off the signboard on either end, hovering in space. The organic shapes of philodendron leaves and the celebratory starbursts of palm tree fronds in the sky place the architecture in its full context. Linton's exaggerated perspective adds energy but does not distort the design's mastery of scale and formal power over the suburban landscape.

| Rendering by Lee Linton | Built; demolished

7079 Sunset Blvd., Hollywood

CAROLINA PINES JR. RESTAURANT (CONCEPT)
Los Angeles, 1955

An earlier version of the restaurant on the previous spread instead places the outdoor dining area against a mosaic tile mural wall and under a different sign solution. Here, the sign's letters, boldly three-dimensional, float above the colorful wall, which is ornamented with artwork of abstracted fish. At night, indirect light spills from behind the letters to make the sign even more prominent. Linton's drawing, set on busy La Brea Avenue, captures the mise-en-scène of an urban space on the modern commercial strip.

ENTIRE FACIA OF BACKLIGHTED PLASTIC (YELLOW)

ARMET & DAVIS AIA ARCHITECTS   SEPT
1344 WILSHIRE BLVD.   LOS ANGELES

Linton's renderings offer a delightful tour of the building. His style conveys the strengths of Googie—the building's vivid presence, landscaped outdoor dining, and popularity. Linton welcomes the viewer in with abstracted but stylish figures that move through the space. Curving soffits inside echo the curves of the roof outside, uniting indoors and outdoors aesthetically. Modern artwork on panels, lighting fixtures, and signage accent the architecture.
| *Rendering by Lee Linton*

CAROLINA PINES JR. COFFEE SHOP
Fullerton, California, 1956

| Client: Mahaca Inc. | Rendering by Lee Linton

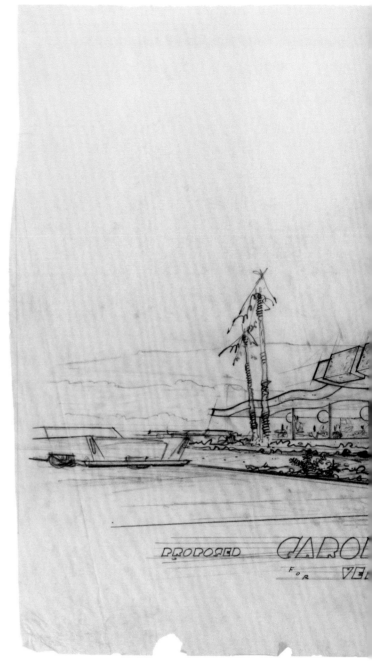

CAROLINA PINES JR. #2
Los Angeles, 1961

Two design studies, for sites in Fullerton (top left) and on Vermont Avenue (above), use the sine-wave folded-plate roofline from previous incarnations. This concept evolved into the thin-shell concrete roof design, later constructed of wood and plaster for budgetary reasons, that was eventually built on Vermont [see the following spread].
| Client: Vermont Company | Rendering by Lee Linton

1·28·61

SCHEME 3

CAROLINA PINES JR

VERMONT NEAR SIXTH

CAROLINA PINES JR. #2
Los Angeles, 1961

ARMET & DAVIS A.I.A. ARCHITECTS
2440 WEST THIRD STREET
LOS ANGELES 57, CALIFORNIA

The organic character of the roof over the Carolina Pines Jr. on Vermont Avenue was underscored by curving counter-arches rising from the earth to match the roofline, uniting high-tech design and autochthonous landscape.
| *Rendering by Lee Linton*
| *Built; demolished*

CAROLINA-HOLLYWOOD MOTEL
OWNER: IRVING SUTTER COMPANY.
ARMET & DAVIS A.I.A. ARCHITECTS

CAROLINA-HOLLYWOOD MOTEL
Los Angeles, 1957

Though also Modern in style, this motel, built adjacent to the Carolina Pines Jr. on La Brea, reflects the modular, rectilinear aspects so typical of a 1950s motel.

| Owner: Irving Sutter Company | Built; altered

CAROLINA PINES JR.
encino
for: mrs charley foy

ARMET & DAVIS AIA
architects ... los angeles

CAROLINA PINES JR. #3
Encino, California, 1965

| Client: Mrs. Charley Foy | Built; demolished

ROMEO'S TIMES SQUARE RESTAURANT

Los Angeles, c. 1955

ROMEO'S TIMES SQUARE RESTAURANT
Los Angeles, c. 1955

Both of these drawings, for Romeo's Times Square (later Johnie's) and Sierra Inn, are undated, so it cannot be determined which came first. Nonetheless, each sports a butterfly roof lifted on stone-clad pillars rising from the earth, with a broad structural facade that comfortably accommodates the integrated signage. They are worth comparing here for the different choices made in important details. For example, the larger Sierra Inn, at right, has an open-air forecourt, whereas the smaller Romeo's creates the same sense of openness to the exterior with a well-detailed corner of glass (above, at center) that allows customers sitting inside to feel as if they are outdoors.

| Client: H. S. Ahrens & Montgomery Holding Co. | Rendering by Lee Linton | Built; standing

for MR H.S. AHRENS & MONTGOMERY HOLDING CO.
ARMET & DAVIS ARCHITECTS 1344 WILSHIRE BLVD

WOODY HOLDER'S SIERRA INN RESTAURANT
c. 1955

| Client: John M. Stahl | Rendering by Lee Linton

woody holder's "SIERRA INN" RESTAURANT · washington blvd. at anaheim road
MR. JOHN M. STAHL · OWNER
ARMET & DAVIS AIA ARCHITECTS

PEN AND QUILL RESTAURANT IN MANHATTAN BEACH FOR MR. R. DEUBE

PEN & QUILL ENTRANCE   ARMET & DAVIS A.I.A. ARCHITECTS.

PEN AND QUILL RESTAURANT
Manhattan Beach, California, 1955

Armet & Davis's formal architectural vocabulary fits within the spectrum of mid-century Modernism: abstracted geometric shapes contrasted with open screens, dropped soffits with free-form cutouts accented with artful Modern decorative lighting, hanging stairs, and indoor planters, as shown in the color sketch at left. Nonetheless, they rarely directly imitate the work of famous architects like Richard Neutra or Oscar Niemeyer; the firm's designs are original and highly studied, as the Norm's sketches [pages 68-77] indicate. Embracing their commercial functions, the buildings' forms often follow signage, and their bold scale is appropriate for that demanded by the automobile and its growing popularity.

| Client: R. Rubens | Rendering by Lee Linton | Built; demolished

GOOGIES
1955

555 W. 5th St., Los Angeles

GOOGIES DOWNTOWN (REMODEL)
Los Angeles, 1955

The original Googies restaurant on the Sunset Strip, from which the architectural genre takes its name, was designed by John Lautner in 1949. In 1955, Googies opened a second location, in downtown Los Angeles, designed by Armet & Davis, shown at right. Though it uses the same corrugated-metal decking for its roofline, it is in fact a remodel of the ground-floor commercial space of an existing hotel on Pershing Square and not a freestanding structure.
| Built; demolished

These sketches show two alternative designs considered for the downtown Googies on the previous spread. The study above plays with perspective and depth by running standing seams on a triangular roof form, suggesting an A-frame roofline akimbo that riffs on Frank Lloyd Wright's Unitarian Meeting House, in Madison, Wisconsin (1951). Though the flaps appear to be three-dimensional, they are actually in the same plane. Unique to this design is the triangulated-metal window mullions of the broad glass wall. Clear and opaque panes in diamond and arrowhead shapes create an original geometric pattern reminiscent of Wright's glass window art from his Prairie houses, or the ornamental panels in later houses by Eugene Masselink, an apprentice of Wright's. Here, the panes are scaled up to draw attention to a busy urban corner. The hotel's existing structural columns are clad in mosaic tile. Note the repeating, distinctive Googies logo on the clear glass front door.

More radical in its geometry, the study above uses prominently angled columns and a slanting spear-head roofline to indicate an off-kilter kineticism. Inside, on the far wall above the counter behind the rhythmic line of coral-colored stools, another, thinner soffit creates an asymmetrical zigzag counterpoint to the main roofline outside. Note the handwritten instructions by Eldon Davis to the designer.

The rendering above is done in an impressionistic style—loose, suggestive, colorful. Applying the opaque color of tempera or grease pencil over graphite, the artist (probably Lee Linton) conveys the lively tones and energetic lines as well as the commotion of busy diners in a popular restaurant.

With its slanting roof folded down to form a sun flap over the sidewalk, then flipped up at the opposite end, this remodel design is unmistakably Googie in both style and name. Similar functional sun flaps facing toward the western afternoon sun were a motif of Modern houses by A. Quincy Jones and Palmer and Krisel; the line between high-art and commercial designs was never as distinct as critics thought. The gray angled pylon, at far left in the above sketch, echoes Lautner's plastered (read: concrete) pylon on the Sunset Strip Googies. This is very possibly a nod to establishing a common Googies "look."

Graphically, Linton's bold lines show the speed and confidence with which he made his renderings. He knew what the drawing and the building needed to express: movement, a visual cue to the front door, a secondary soffit inside as shelter over the counter stools, and plenty of texture, color, and line to lead the eye. For all its variety, the work holds its own as a unified composition fulfilling the practical function to draw in customers and make them comfortable as they enjoy their meal.

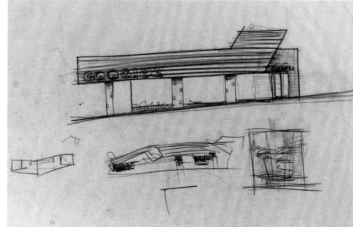

A study sketch investigates colors, roof forms, and sign placement

"GARDEN ROOM" — TRUMAN'S RESTAURANT RENOVATION
ARMET & DAVIS, AIA, ARCHITECTS   15 JULY 1955

"GARDEN ROOM" — TRUMAN'S RESTAURANT RENOVATION
ARMET & DAVIS, AIA, ARCHITECTS   18 JULY 1955

On this spread are two design choices for a new Garden Room update to the existing Spanish-style Truman's Drive-In and Dining Room at Wilshire and Westwood Boulevards in West Los Angeles. The first, shown above, features a Mesoamerican motif of Aztec or Mayan ornament; the centerpiece is a statue inside a circular glass case in the middle of the room. The sketch at left, is more subdued, with more abstracted ornaments.

| Rendering by Lee Linton

Original artwork was a key element of most Armet & Davis coffee shops. The sketch at right shows a detail of a five-foot-tall sculpture of a bird. Labels on the drawing call out the piece's craftsmanship: "braised brass rods and plexiglass plumage," "textured plexiglass and metal rib cage," "hammered stainless steel or nickel plate."

| Rendering by Lee Linton
| Built; demolished

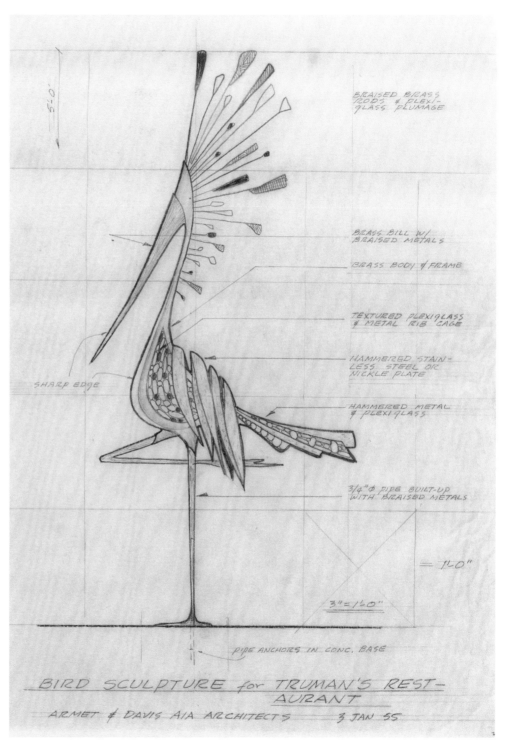

BRAISED BRASS RODS & PLEXI-GLASS PLUMAGE

BRASS BILL W/ BRAISED METALS

BRASS BODY & FRAME

TEXTURED PLEXIGLASS & METAL RIB CAGE

HAMMERED STAIN-LESS STEEL OR NICKLE PLATE

HAMMERED METAL & PLEXIGLASS

SHARP EDGE

3/4"Ø PIPE BUILT-UP WITH BRAISED METALS

= 1'-0"

3" = 1'-0"

PIPE ANCHORS IN CONC. BASE

BIRD SCULPTURE for TRUMAN'S REST-AURANT

ARMET & DAVIS AIA ARCHITECTS   3 JAN 55

TEDDY'S DRIVE-IN
Los Angeles, 1955

The Modern archetype of the Los Angeles drive-in, first developed in the 1930s, continues here. In the drawing above, drive-in service is sheltered by a wide canopy. The kitchen is located centrally for convenient access. Indoor seating is to the left, and a strip-scaled sign above it all informs motorists. Helen Fong's interior design, in the sketch opposite, incorporates different wall materials and ceiling treatments—natural stone, ceramic tiles, translucent plastic panels, and a hanging planter in sync with the geometry on the drive-in canopy outside—to create a Modern space.

| *Rendering by Lee Linton*

DINING ROOM

TEDDY'S DRIVE-IN

ARMET & DAVIS, ARCHITECTS
4 APRIL 55

RESTAURANT for MR NALDER   ARMET & DAVIS A.I.A ARCHITECTS

YUMMIE'S
1955

Indoor dining in a garden room environment surrounded by glass, exhibition cooking with counter seating, a self-service window, and outdoor dining are all combined under a dynamic roofline.
| Client: Mr. Nalder

ARROW SQUARE　SHOPPING CENTER · COVINA · CALIFORNIA

WILLIAM VANDER PLOEG · OWNER　ARMET & DAVIS · ARCHITECTS · AIA · LOS ANGELES

ARROW SQUARE SHOPPING CENTER
Covina, California, 1955

A two-story shopping mall in Covina is designed to include a variety of stores, an open-air pedestrian mall, and plenty of parking. Note the market anchoring the left end, and the coffee shop with a distinctive roof on the right.
| Client: William Vander Ploeg

"PIX" COFFEE SHOP

"PIX" COFFEE SHOP VOORHIS & DAVIS A.I.A. ARCHITECTS for JACK L. WACHS OWNER

PIX COFFEE SHOP
Los Angeles, 1956

The design for Pix, shown at left, represents a catalog of Googie architecture's spatial, structural, and decorative elements. Decorative screens, at far left, shield one of the interior dining spaces from car traffic. Cone-shaped columns are clad in colorful ceramic tiles, and palm trees grow through holes cut into the soffit. A tapered truss roof floats over the mostly open, glassy interior. Another version of the design, in color with a gullwing roof seen at bottom left, shows how the artwork adds to the dazzle.

| Client: Jack A. Wachs | Rendering by Lee Linton | Built; altered

10531 S. Western Ave., Los Angeles

HOLLY'S
Hawthorne, California, 1956

Here, the three-dimensional letters in "Holly's" become one with the architecture, melding structure and signage. The north end, facing oncoming traffic on Hawthorne Boulevard, draws attention through its distinctive roof form, which has been tilted up to create a high-ceilinged dining area, while the rest of the building stretches southward along the commercial strip.

| Client: Jack A. Wachs | Rendering by Lee Linton | Built; demolished

13765 Hawthorne Blvd., Hawthorne

DIMY'S COFFEE SHOP
Long Beach, California, 1956

1600 Pacific Coast Highway, Long Beach

In contrast to much of today's architecturally lazy commercial architecture, each functional element of Googie is a sharply defined part of a well-composed whole. Stop's (named Dimy's when it opened) is proof. Among these elements are Stop's unmistakable roofline, supported by oversize I-beam columns with circular web lighteners, evoking a rocket gantry launching pad; the space-age sign overhead; the palm trees and torch lily flowers of the exterior; the inside counter, presided over by toque-crowned chefs holding court in front of shiny pie cases; and the table-seating area, shown at far right in the drawing. Each element is given its own appropriate form, yet together they present a clear symbolism appealing to a modern mid-century public amazed by (and enjoying) new ways of life courtesy of technology, television, freeways, space travel, computers, and miniature transistor radios. Lee Linton's deft hand brings life and energy to match the architecture. This is a large drawing, 3 by 4 feet. Its wide panorama establishes the building's position on the commercial strip and allows the viewer to wander in through the front door before pivoting to find a seat at the counter or at a booth or table. (Incidentally, in Linton's drawings the counter is always full, the sign of a popular restaurant.) The oblique lines of sidewalks, curbs, and streets lead the eye into the distance. The perspective is dramatic, matching the horizontal vista of the suburban commercial strip. A finned car parked in front completes the image: a suburban setting that combines the large scale of the car culture with the intimate scale of the counter stool.
| Client: Sunset Oil Co. | Rendering by Lee Linton | Built; demolished

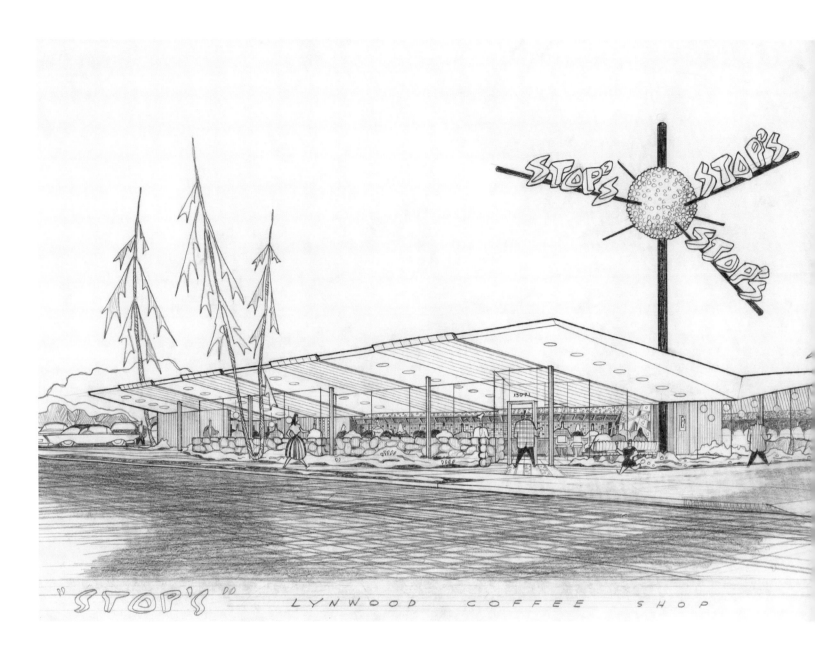

"STOP'S" COFFEE SHOP
Lynwood, California, 1956

The sign was an essential part of a Googie design, so before a client settled on a name, "Stop's" was sometimes used as a placeholder to show how the building and sign related as an integral concept.
| Rendering by Lee Linton

MET. & DAVIS, A.I.A.,
ARCHITECTS
S ANGELES, CALIF.

YORBA LINDA RANCH & COUNTRY CLUB
Yorba Linda, California, 1956

Forest Smith, Armet & Davis's client for the firm's first restaurant project, Clock, also commissioned country clubs.
| Client: Forest G. Smith

FALCON
Inglewood, California, 1956

By highlighting two vanishing points, this Lee Linton drawing, top, focuses on the billboard scale of the upturned roofline at left in the sketch, and on the long cantilever emerging from and anchored by the angular, windowless block on the right. While most signage fonts designed by Armet & Davis were Modern, the contrasting Gothic font used here evokes the ancient sport of falconry.

| Owner: Louis Lesser | Client: P.A. Smith, Loyd S. Pettegrew, and Lou Barnes | Rendering by Lee Linton

PROPOSED 96 UNIT MOTEL
MANHATTAN BEACH, CALIF.
ARMET & DAVIS A.I.A. ARCHITECTS

MOTEL SAFARI
Manhattan Beach, California, 1956

Like that of coffee shops, the design of motels was also a response to the growth of the car culture and thus shared similar forms, scale, and siting. The Motel Safari, next to the Pen and Quill restaurant [page 90], demonstrates how the forms, materials, and rooflines of a Googie restaurant could be expanded to define a multi-building complex. This concept would be used again for the Ellis Motel, in Calexico [page 186].

DENNY'S RESTAURANTS
1955–1966

DANNY'S COFFEE SHOPS

ARMET & DAVIS A.I.A. ARCHITECTS
2440 WEST THIRD STREET
LOS ANGELES, CALIFORNIA

DANNY'S COFFEE SHOPS
1957

Denny's (originally Danny's) cycled through several designs before hitting on a prototype [page 116].

DANNY'S COFFEE SHOP no. 11, long beach
FOR MR. HAROLD BUTLER   ARMET & DAVIS, A.I.A, ARCHITECTS

DANNY'S COFFEE SHOP #11
Long Beach, California, 1957

Client Harold Butler, founder of Denny's, asked for different alternatives over the years, including a mid-block site bracketed by other buildings instead of a freestanding building surrounded by a parking lot. Compare Danny's #11, in Long Beach, shown above, with a similar solution for a Norm's location [page 77].

| Client: Harold Butler

DENNY'S COFFEE SHOP
HAROLD BUTLER ENTERPRISES   ARMET & DAVIS A.I.A. ARCHITECTS

DENNY'S COFFEE SHOP #94 (PROTOTYPE)
Various locations, 1957

This prototype design, first built in Anaheim and West Covina in 1957, would soon spawn restaurants coast to coast as the chain expanded. It is a classic Googie design, with a boomerang-shaped roofline balanced on a stone pylon to create an energetic, asymmetrical interior space surrounded by glass walls.
| Client: Harold Butler Enterprises | Built; prototype design

foothill motel and Denny's restaurant AUBURN, CALIFORNIA
for Mr. Pat Train

ARMET & DAVIS AIA architects

FOOTHILL MOTEL AND DENNY'S RESTAURANT
Auburn, California, 1959

Several expanded Denny's designs by Armet & Davis were combined with the firm's designs for motels in Auburn and Palm Springs, as well as Reno, Nevada, and other locations.
| Client: Pat Train | Built; prototype design

Denny's

RESTAURAN

For HAROLD BL

125 SEATS
ENTERPRISES

a.7 ARMET & DAVIS AIA
architects ... los angeles
4-4-66

DENNY'S #2 (PROTOTYPE)
Various locations, 1966

This second prototype design replaced the first as the Denny's chain continued to expand. The design and drawing were the work of future Armet Davis Newlove partner, Victor Newlove, under the direction of Helen Fong.

| Client: Harold Butler Enterprises | Rendering by Victor Newlove | Built; prototype design

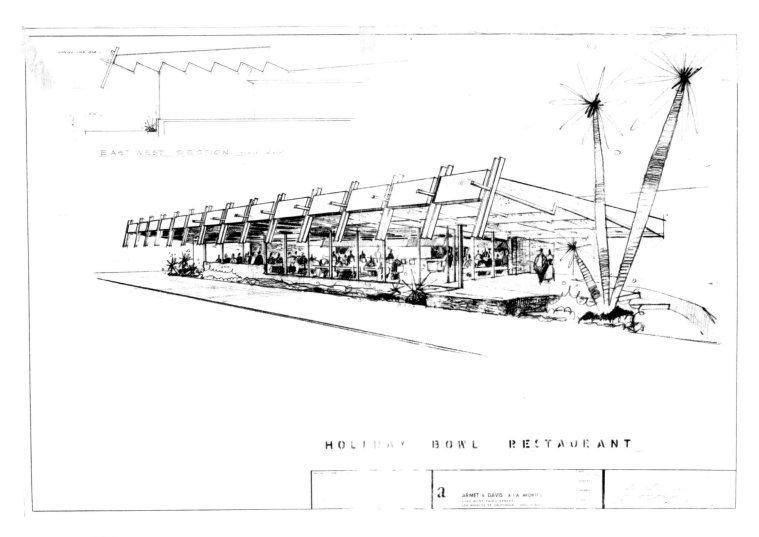

HOLIDAY BOWL RESTAURANT
Los Angeles, 1956

The Holiday Bowl and restaurant served members of the large Japanese American community in L.A.'s Crenshaw district.
| Built; coffee shop altered; bowling alley demolished | Top; Rendering by Lee Linton, Above; rendering by T.W. Kowalski

SAKAI APARTMENTS, MOTEL, AND RESTAURANT
1957

| Client: Mr. and Mrs. George M. Sakai | Rendering by Purciel & Nicholl

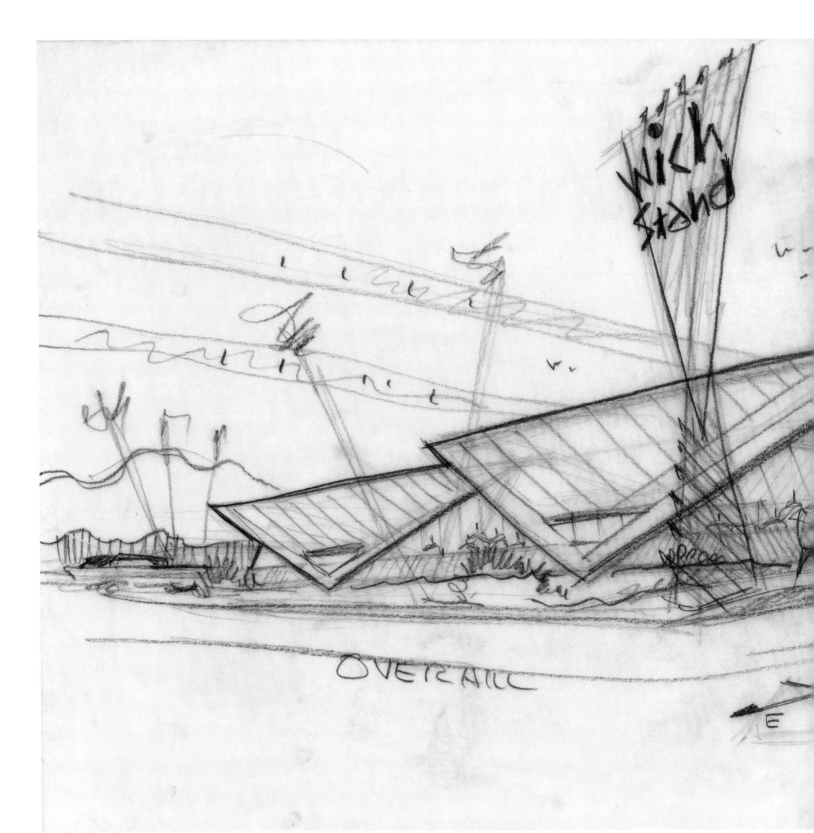

WICH
stand

OVERALL

E

THE WICH STAND
Los Angeles, 1957

The owners of the Wich Stand, like those of other drive-ins originating in the 1930s, felt compelled to update the restaurant's image in the post-war boom with a Modern design. This early sketch, at left, shows two A-frame shells nestled one into the other, allowing views and natural sunlight to enter where they overlap. As in other Modern designs, the window is treated not as a hole punched in a wall (as in historical architecture) but as the void created between structural elements. Indeed, the building has no walls; the roof touches the ground. A canted wall, at right in the drawing, provides a horizontal counterpoint to the roof. Far from the minimalist International Style, this design and others by Armet & Davis clearly branch from the Organic architecture of Frank Lloyd Wright, Bruce Goff, John Lautner, Mackie and Kamrath, and others. As built [see the promotional materials below], the Wich Stand used an upward-slanting cantilevered roof pinned down by an angled-spear sign and anchored by a solid stone buttress— the Googie motif of high-tech roof contrasting with rugged stone form rising from the earth. Compare to the coffee shop at the Sakai Apartments, Motel, and Restaurant [page 121]. | Rendering (left) by Lee Linton | Built version (below); altered

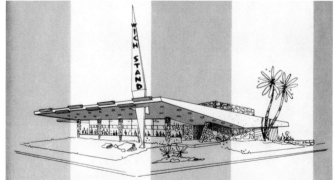

THE WICH STAND

FIGUEROA AT FLORENCE • SLAUSON AT OVERHILL • LOS ANGELES

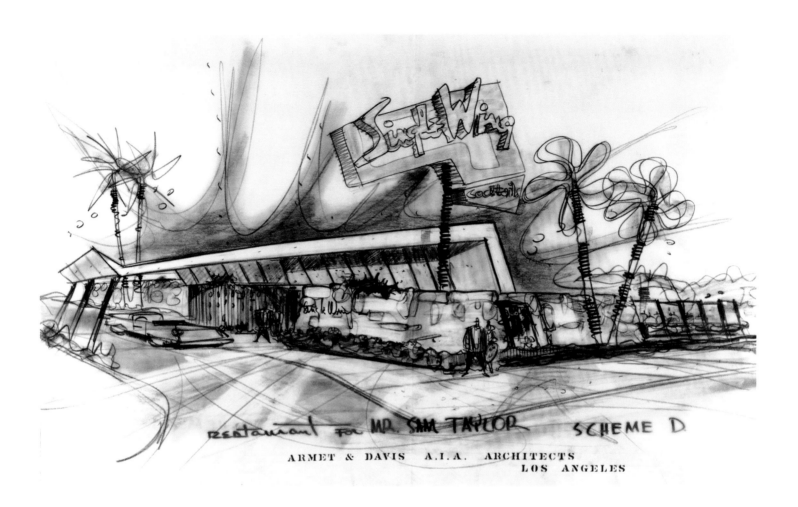

Restaurant for MR. SAM TAYLOR   SCHEME D

ARMET & DAVIS A.I.A. ARCHITECTS
LOS ANGELES

SINGLE WING
c. 1957

This Lee Linton rendering hints at the fluid syntax of Googie design in shaping space. The battered wall begins at left with freeform artwork, becomes a curving wall to guide guests to the front door, announces the restaurant name at center, and, at far right, transforms into a screen of steel I-beams enclosing an outdoor dining area. Above the stone wall hovers a crisply tapered porte cochere canopy.
| Client: Sam Taylor | Rendering by Lee Linton

RESTAURANT COFFEE SHOP DRIVE-IN TUCSON, ARIZ. JACOME INC OWNER
ARMET & DAVIS A.I.A. ARCHITECTS FRANK K. JOHNSON LESSEE

BIG 6 RESTAURANT, COFFEE SHOP, AND DRIVE-IN
Tucson, Arizona, c. 1957

In Googie architecture, each building function is given a distinct, appropriate form. Together, they are unified into a balanced composition—this is what makes Googie Modern. Here, the main dining room is fronted by sun flaps and an expanse of glass to open it to the street and landscaping. In California Modern residences, the glass wall was a feature turned to an exterior view or a private garden; in this commercial building, the transparent wall is turned to the street, intentionally allowing the interior of the restaurant itself to become the view as seen by motorists. The windowless block, at left in the rendering, holds either banquet rooms, a lounge, or a kitchen. The sign, visible from afar, is situated over the front door to mark the entry point.

| Owner: Jacome Inc. | Client: Frank K. Johnson | Rendering by Lee Linton

BIG BOY COFFEE SHOPS

1960–1974

BOB'S BIG BOY COFFEE SHOP (PROTOTYPE)
Long Beach, California, 1960

ARMET & DAVIS A.I.A. ARCHITECTS
2440 WEST THIRD STREET
LOS ANGELES 57, CALIFORNIA

As now-famous chains like Bob's Big Boy and Denny's expanded across the country, prototype designs helped to establish the brand identity wherever new restaurants were built. The roofline of the new Big Boy prototype was a clean, sweeping curve cantilevering from a solid, patterned concrete block counterbalance at the rear, expressing a combined structural logic. Armet & Davis's design for Mel's [page 151] from 1957 anticipated this formal concept. Walls and columns clad with natural stone lead the eye to the glassy entry. The rendering style is crisply Modern, with a deft use of line weight to focus attention on key features including the sign, the entry, and the interior decor..
| Client: Robert C. Wian Enterprises | Rendering by Don Hocker | Built; prototype design

FRISCH'S - BIG BOY COFFEE S
FOR BENNETT ENTERPRISES   ARMET & DAVIS AIA

FRISCH'S BIG BOY COFFEE SHOP & DRIVE-IN
Toledo, Ohio, 1957

& DRIVE - IN   TOLEDO , OHIO

ITECTS   LOS ANGELES   57 ,   CALIF.   11-

In other regions, Wian franchised Big Boy restaurants to companies such as Azar's, Blazo's, Manners, Elias Bros., and Frisch's. Those companies usually came to Armet & Davis to design restaurants distinctive to their regions. This Frisch's Big Boy, in Toledo, shows how the basic Googie motifs (prominent roofline, sign, natural stone pillars with glass walls) evolved over time. The blending of a centralized pentagonal pavilion with a lower, longer folded roof builds on ideas formulated by Frank Lloyd Wright.

| Client: Bennett Enterprises | Rendering by Don Hocker

BOB'S BIG BOY
Washington, DC, c. 1957

This Wian Bob's Big Boy, above, features a roof similar to that of Pann's in Inglewood, but was intended for Washington, DC.
| Rendering by Lee Linton

"CBOY" COFFEE SHOP WASHINGTON D.C.
ARMET & DAVIS A.I.A. ARCHITECTS.

Bob's
BIG BOY FAMILY RESTAURANT   FRESNO, CALIF.

ARMET & DAVIS A1A
architects ... los angeles

BOB'S BIG BOY FAMILY RESTAURANT
Fresno, California, c. 1962

The two tapered, perpendicular spires supporting the sign of this Bob's in Fresno, shown in the color sketch at top, became a standard feature of the curved-roof prototypes for Bob's Big Boy restaurants. Note the roof's geometry echoed in the battered wall at left side (see detail, above) in either wood or mosaic tile. | *Built; prototype design*

MARK'S COFFEE SHOP
Washington, DC, 1958

Armet & Davis's designs evolved in different directions. The lower profile of this Mark's Big Boy, in Washington, DC, is done on a more residential scale, whereas Frisch's Big Boy designs in Ohio and Florida grew out of the earlier Googie designs highlighting bold roofs. Roof trusses are emphasized by depicting exaggerated beam ends along the edge. This motif begins with Norm's but becomes even more pronounced in these later designs. The design serves the same function of making the buildings noticeable on crowded commercial strips.

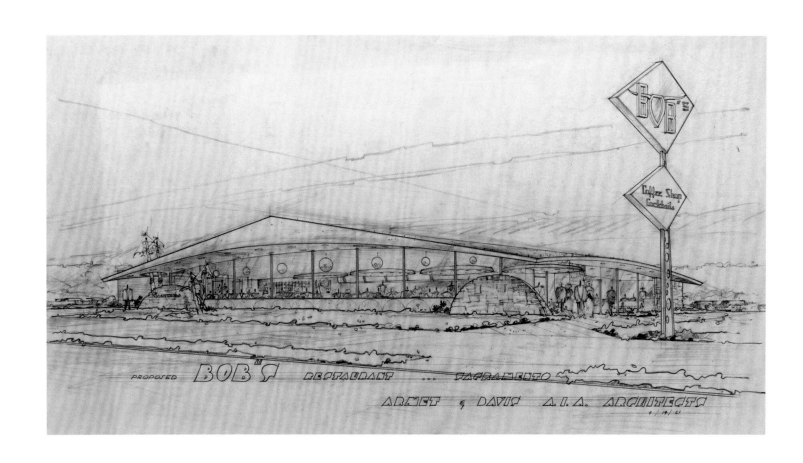

BOB'S RESTAURANT
Sacramento, California, 1961

Sporting a unique logo that departs radically from that of Bob's Big Boy, and featuring an added cocktail lounge, this Sacramento design may not have been for a restaurant in Wian's chain. Nevertheless, the curving brow-like roofline, repeated in circular dropped soffits inside, shows yet another exploration of architectural geometries defining exterior structure and interior space.

AZAR'S BIG BOY, SCHEME I
Fort Wayne, Indiana, 1960

Two Azar's Big Boy alternative designs unite indoors and out using extended colonnades of steel I-beam spider legs or angled panels. Compare to the spider-leg beams for Stanley Burke's [page 153, lower right].

SCHEME II

AUG 12/60

AZAR'S BIG BOY, SCHEME II
Fort Wayne, Indiana, 1960

PROPOSED BIG BOY AZARS SCHEME II
FORT WAYNE INDIANA

ARNET & DAVIS A.I.A. ARCHITECTS

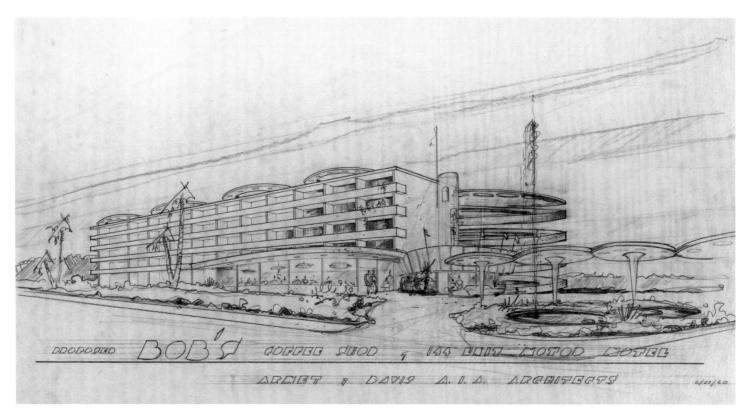

BOB'S COFFEE SHOP & MOTOR HOTEL
1960

This unusual proposal combined a Bob's coffee shop with a five-story motor inn. The circular penthouses and lily pad canopies show an Organic Modern influence, perhaps referencing Frank Lloyd Wright's Bramlett Motor Hotel (1956). Though they used Wright's vocabulary, Armet & Davis did not simply copy his design; here, they added a spiral ramp at the rear (shown in the top sketch) to allow guests to drive to their rooms on the upper floors. | *Not built*

BLAZO'S BIG BOY COFFEE SHOP & CURB SERVICE
armet & davis a.i.a. architects   los angeles, california
jahr-anderson-machida associates   dearborn, michigan

BLAZO'S BIG BOY COFFEE SHOP
Dearborn, Michigan, 1961

For a typical suburban parking lot setting, Blazo's in Michigan turned to the dramatic A-frame roof with glass infill that Armet & Davis fashioned in an early Huddle proposal [page 48–49].

KIP'S   BIG BOY   DRIVE-IN   RESTA

FOR KEN C. BEMIS

KIP'S BIG BOY DRIVE-IN RESTAURANT
Oklahoma City, 1961

At Kip's, represented in the sketch at right, sculptural supports, possibly of wood or concrete, for the car canopies shelter the drive-in service and create a vivid architectural statement for a utilitarian structure.

| Client: Ken C. Bemis

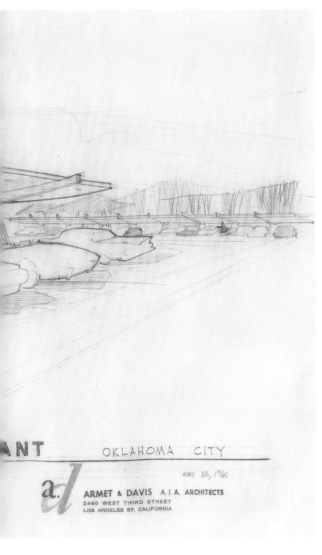

OKLAHOMA CITY

MAY 25, 1961

a.d

ARMET & DAVIS A.I.A. ARCHITECTS
2440 WEST THIRD STREET
LOS ANGELES 57, CALIFORNIA

FOR BENNETT ENTERPRISES TOLEDO, OHIO

d ARCHITECTS · LOS ANGELES, CALIF.

FRISCH'S BIG BOY COFFEE SHOP
Toledo, Ohio, 1962

| Client: Bennett Enterprises

BIG BOY PORTFOLIO *139*

AZAR'S BIG BOY COFFEE SHOP
Fort Wayne, Indiana, 1961

Azar's Big Boy reinterprets Googie for an atypical urban downtown setting.

BOB'S BIG BOY COFFEE SHOP

Armet & Davis A.I.A. Architects
los angeles, calif.

BOB'S BIG BOY COFFEE SHOP
c. 1962

Though this A-frame design was never built, its detail warrants a closer look. At left, the dining room space, with its high ceiling, contrasts with the lower, sloped ceiling at right. The panels between the windows contain stained glass, which is echoed in the custom-designed chandeliers inside. Low, tilted stone walls root the building to the earth amid lush landscaping.
| *Rendering by Afred M. Gordon* | *Not built*

BOB'S BIG BOY COFFEE SHOP
c 1962

As at Pann's, the geometry of the broad, sheltering turtle-shell roof is emphasized by concentric bands of multi-colored stone.
| Client: Robert C. Wian Enterprises | Built; prototype design

FRISCH'S HARTWELL **BIG BOY COFFEE SHOP**
for: STANLEY FRISCH

CINCINNATI, OHIO
ARMET & DAVIS AIA ARCHITECTS

FRISCH'S HARTWELL BIG BOY COFFEE SHOP
Cincinnati, 1962

Note the inventive variations on expressive structural systems here and on pages 138-140, as seen in the designs for Kip's Big Boy in Oklahoma City, Frisch's Big Boy in Toledo, Azar's Big Boy in Fort Wayne, and others.
| Client: Stanley Frisch

FRISCH'S **BIG BOY** COFFEE SHOP INDIANAPOLIS, INDIANA
For FREDERICK COREY

ARMET & DAVIS A.I.A. ARCHITECTS
Los Angeles, Calif.

FRISCH'S BIG BOY COFFEE SHOP
Indianapolis, 1962

| Client: Frederick Corey | Rendering by Alfred M. Gordon

FRISCH'S *big boy* COFFEE SHOP Tampa, Florida
for: Richard Pasch & Dan Linder

ARMET & DAVIS A.I.A Architect
los angeles. calif

FRISCH'S BIG BOY COFFEE SHOP
Tampa, Florida, 1962

| Client: Richard Pasch and Dan Linder

MANNERS COFFEE SHOP
Cleveland, Ohio, 1962

| Client: Manners Restaurant & Enterprises | Rendering by Don Hocker

PLEASANT VALLEY SHOPPING CENTER — CLEVELAND, OHIO
2440 W. 3RD STREET   LOS ANGELES 57   CALIFORNIA   JANUARY 8, 1962

The chiseled roofline of Manners Big Boy in Cleveland is repeated in the tripartite roadside sign, hoisted on a steel I-beam featuring circular holes known as web lighteners. The "Auto-Order" service portion of the restaurant, seen at right toward the back of the building, complements the architecture, from its stone podium to its wedge-shaped canopy. Everything, from the contemporary cars to the neighboring Pleasant Valley Shopping Center and Space Age gas station, reflects the optimism of mid-century Modernism.

Kip's BIG BOY FAMILY RESTAURANT, DALLAS/HOUSTON
for Fred Bell Enterprises

ARMET & DAVIS AIA
architects ... los angeles

KIP'S BIG BOY FAMILY RESTAURANT
Dallas/Houston, 1965

| Client: Fred Bell Enterprises

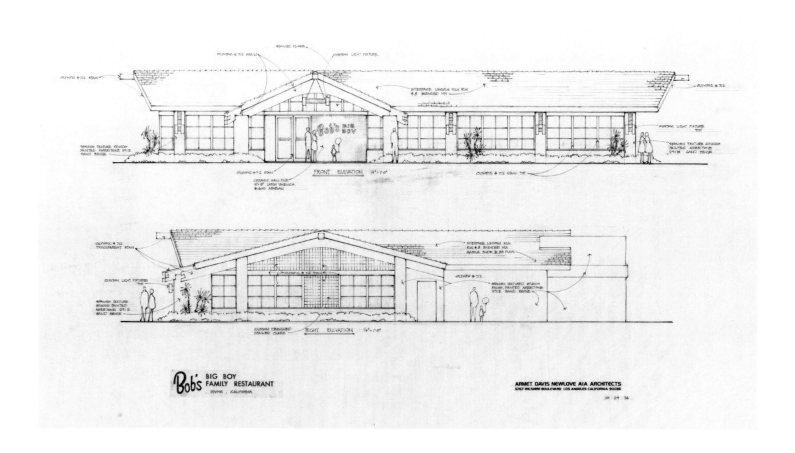

FRONT ELEVATION

RIGHT ELEVATION

Bob's BIG BOY
FAMILY RESTAURANT
IRVINE, CALIFORNIA

ARMET DAVIS NEWLOVE AIA ARCHITECTS
5767 WILSHIRE BOULEVARD LOS ANGELES CALIFORNIA 90036

BOB'S BIG BOY FAMILY RESTAURANT ("CHULA VISTA" PROTOTYPE)
Irvine, California, 1974

The future of Bob's Big Boy was the Chula Vista model, which marked the transition from Googie Modern to a more low-key, residential profile for the California coffee shop. This prototype was widely successful and featured colorful custom-designed stained glass in the clerestory windows.

| Rendering by Victor Newlove | Built; prototype design

ARMSTRONG NURSERY
Ontario, California, 1956

ARMSTRONG NURSERY
Ontario, California, 1957

Plant nurseries became signatures of suburban California as owners sought innovative landscaping for their new tract homes. Trellised canopies and model planting beds were often part of these designs (see Raphael Soriano's Hallawell Seed Co., San Francisco, 1942), but Armet & Davis expanded on this idea by interspersing enclosed pavilions to be used as salesrooms. The Armstrong Nursery chain was a steady client, and the 1956 Ontario location (shown at top) used the arresting A-frame form to turn the nursery into a visual landmark.
| Client: Armstrong Nurseries Inc.
| Built; prototype design

COFFEE SHOP for mr. and mrs. mel bustram, oxnard · armet and davis, aia architects

1041 S. Oxnard Blvd.,
Oxnard

MEL'S COFFEE SHOP
Oxnard, California, 1957

An early color design sketch for Mel's coffee shop, shown at top, captures the kinetic energy of the cars, visuals, and pace of the mid-twentieth-century suburban metropolis.
| Client: Mr. and Mrs. Mel Bustram | Rendering by Lee Linton | Built; altered

Stanley Burkes Coffee Shop by armet & davis aia architects · homer e.

STANLEY BURKE'S COFFEE SHOP
Los Angeles, 1958

Theoretically, this extraordinary folded-plate roof proposal (above) is buildable; the peaks and valleys work together to create a structure stiffer than that of a flat-plane roof. It also shapes the interior space, forming a higher ceiling on the left, above the counter seating, and a lower ceiling on the right, above the tables and banquette seating. While the figures and sense of narrative energy appear to be those of Lee Linton, the drawing's free-flowing lines (probably suggesting the mountainous rim of L.A.'s San Fernando Valley) and the pattern of the abstract trees are unique to the Armet & Davis archive. The rendering of Stanley Burke's as built, shown at right, depicts an equally extraordinary catenary curve slung between spider-leg I-beams on either side that is a distinctive feature of the firm's work.

| Owner: Homer E. Fuller | Client: Stanley Burke | Rendering (right) by R. Jackson | Built; extant

, lesson

Stanley Burke's COFFEE SHOP
HOMER E. FULLER - OWNER
ARMET & DAVIS A.I.A. ARCHITECTS

R. Jackson

KING COLE MARKET
ARMSTRONG NURSERIES, INC OWNER
ARMET · DAVIS — AIA ARCHITECTS

KING COLE MARKET
c. 1958

| Owner: Armstrong Nurseries Inc.

Starlite Room   RIVIERA   HOTEL .... LAS   VEGAS

ARMET & DAVIS A.I.A. ARCHITECTS
2440 WEST THIRD STREET
LOS ANGELES 57, CALIFORNIA

STARLITE ROOM, RIVIERA HOTEL
Las Vegas, 1958

The close relationship between Los Angeles's Googie architecture and Las Vegas's architecture is underscored by the fact that many major hotels were designed by coffee shop architects Wayne McAllister, Douglas Honnold, and Martin Stern Jr. Armet & Davis's work in Las Vegas included this proposal for an unusual asymmetrical showroom at the Riviera Hotel featuring massive stone walls flanking the stage. Armet & Davis later designed casinos [pages 190-191] and also built at least three Denny's and a Bob's Big Boy on the Las Vegas Strip and Las Vegas Boulevard South.

/ Client: Riviera Hotel

MELTON'S
c. 1958

As a venue for "Dining / Dancing / Cocktails / Banquet Rooms," Melton's is a different type of restaurant. Note the absence of a glass wall facing the street, though the facade is still full of color, with tiles flanking concrete block panels and double-wood beams establishing an eye-catching rhythm along the street.

| Client: R. Rubens | Rendering by Lee Linton

HUMPHREY'S RESTAURANT
FOR MR. B.W. HULSMAN

ARMET & DAVIS A.I.A. ARCHITECTS
LOS ANGELES.

HUMPHREY'S
c. 1958

While signs such as those for Melton's and Holly's were integrated into the structures themselves, the sign for Humphrey's takes another approach: a freestanding signpost using modern materials—as shown above, an I-beam with holes cut out of the beam's center, or web, to lighten its weight—a distinctive form holding the restaurant's name, original free-form fonts, and, at times, a representational figure to humanize the design.
| Client: B.W. Hulsman | Rendering by Lee Linton

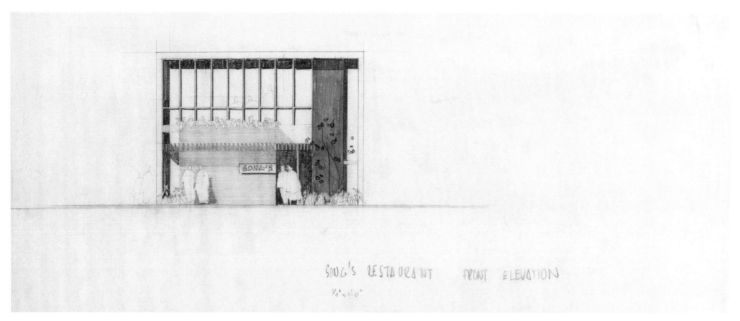

SONG'S RESTAURANT   FRONT ELEVATION

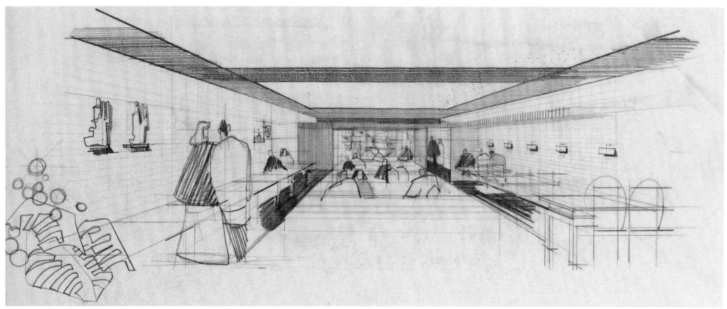

SONG'S RESTAURANT
c. 1958

These drawings, for Song's Restaurant (this page) and the medical offices of the Robert Dench Building (opposite), illustrate how Armet & Davis adjusted their designs for buildings off the commercial strip. The scale of these examples does not need to be enlarged to grab the attention of motorists, yet the Modern rectilinear forms are still handsomely composed.

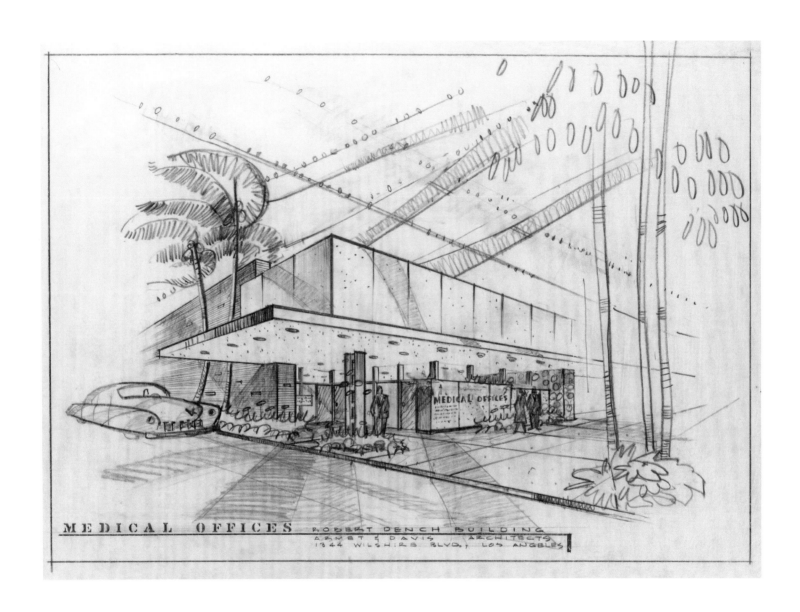

MEDICAL OFFICES, ROBERT DENCH BUILDING
c. 1958

MAR VISTA BOWL AND PEPY'S COCKTAIL LOUNGE
Los Angeles, 1959

Proposals for the Mar Vista Bowl and its adjoining cocktail lounge, Pepy's, include a transformation of the roofline and parapet into a three-dimensional letter "P" (opposite, top). Such motifs blur the line between architecture and signage (also seen in the Carolina Pines Jr., on La Brea [page 79], and the Hollandease restaurant [page 38]) in an architecture of communication.
| Bowl extant; coffee shop demolished

cocktails

plaster

neon letter

full name optional

existing restaurant

abstract pattern in plaster

glass metal & iron deep jambs

flogerete

PEPY'S COCKTAIL LOUNGE
ARMET & DAVIS A.I.A. ARCHITECTS

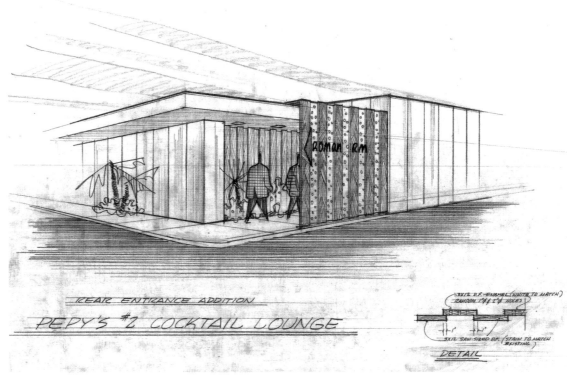

ROMAN RM

REAR ENTRANCE ADDITION

PEPY'S #2 COCKTAIL LOUNGE

3X12 D.F. ENAMEL (WHITE TO MATCH)
RANDOM 1"& 2"ø HOLES

3X12 SAW-SIZED D.F. (STAIN TO MATCH EXISTING)

DETAIL

CHICKEN FRY
c. 1959

The perceived line between themed architecture and mainstream Modern architecture becomes less distinct when it comes to the Chicken Fry restaurant. While its A-frame gables and exposed structural beams are forms that follow function in the standard Modern manner, tiki heads, tapis cloth patterns in the gable ends, and carved animal-head beams capture the Polynesian style popular in mid-century America, derived from historical South Pacific longhouses. The use of themes creates an evocative environment, and Armet & Davis incorporated Tiki, Victorian, Barbary Coast, and other motifs in some of their restaurants and cocktail lounges.

the **Penguin** COFFEE SHOP

BRODRICK PROPERTIES .... OWNER
ALEXANDER & SMITH .... LESSEE

ARMET & DAVIS A.I.A. ARCHITECTS

SEPT. 8/59.

THE PENGUIN COFFEE SHOP
Santa Monica, California, 1959

The modified A-frame roof, introduced at Pann's in 1957, was yet another expressive Modern structure amplified for its suburban commercial strip site. This design reimagines the usually static A-frame as a dynamic, solid form jutting out toward the road, while the glassy prow adds a secondary, transparent element. The cantilevered truss of Norm's and Pix, the butterfly wing of Romeo's Times Square, and the catenary curve of Stanley Burke's all demonstrate Armet & Davis's understanding of Modern form. Though the design is somewhat obligated to Frank Lloyd Wright's Unitarian Meeting House (1951; Madison, Wisconsin), it has been adapted here for a secular roadside purpose. The scale of the oblique bands on the roof, emphasizing its dynamic form, are broader than those on the Wright structure's raised-seam copper roof and suit the car culture's demand for bold lines.

| Owner: Brodrick Properties | Client: Alexander & Smith | Rendering by Lee Linton | Built; restored

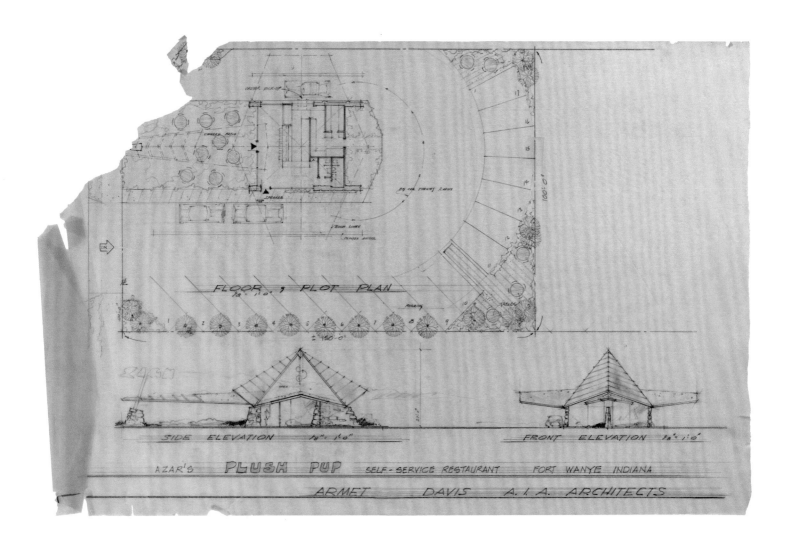

FLOOR & PLOT PLAN

SIDE ELEVATION ⅛"=1'-0"   FRONT ELEVATION ⅛"=1'-0"

AZAR'S PLUSH PUP SELF-SERVICE RESTAURANT FORT WANYE INDIANA

ARMET DAVIS A.I.A. ARCHITECTS

PLUSH PUP SELF-SERVICE RESTAURANT
Fort Wayne, Indiana, c. 1960

An elegantly compact, functional design is governed by the turning radius of a car and, for its midwestern location, a covered outdoor eating area. The delicate geometry of the metal roof with standing seams on the exterior is matched by a tall, open interior space with a chandelier of hanging globes (bottom left in the sketch above). While it taps into the Organic vocabulary of Frank Lloyd Wright, it remains an original concept.

| Rendering by Don Hocker

NEW ENTRY FOR THE TROPICANA LODGE FRESNO, CALIF.
ARMET & DAVIS, A.I.A. ARCHITECTS

NEW ENTRY FOR THE TROPICANA LODGE
Fresno, California, 1960

The contrast between the rough natural stone walls and the slender precision of the proposed glass entry demonstrates the architectural character of Googie design.
| Built, altered

TAHITI RESTAURANT, HALF MOON INN
San Diego, 1960

The restaurant in the color rendering below would later be renamed L'Escale. It is another example of Armet & Davis's blending of Modern and historical South Seas vernacular architecture.

TAHITI restaurant

UNNAMED PROJECT
c 1960

In depicting a structure that could serve as a bowling alley, a large restaurant with cocktail lounge and banquet rooms, a performance venue, or a country club, the sketch above conveys how Googie Modernism gives each possible function its own specific and appropriate interior spaces and exterior forms. The bent steel supports hold the cantilevered entry promenade, at left; the open forecourt welcomes visitors, and windows allow views inside; the large A-frame roof, at center, indicates a large auditorium or hall inside. Note the elegant dress of arriving patrons, lending support to the idea of a performance venue.

STARLITE CLUB
Gardena, California, 1960

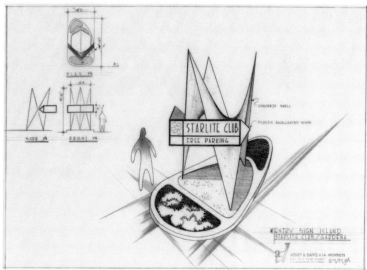

While Armet & Davis's work focused primarily on coffee shops, school and church buildings, and residences, a project such as the Starlite Club links the firm's work to broader architectural concerns of the time. In the rendering at left, note the colorful mosaic tile at the grand entrance. A fountain featuring abstract sculpture, shown in the detail at top, blends with the sculptural structure of the building. A metaphorical starburst tops a pole overhead.

| Rendering by Siegfried Knop | Not built

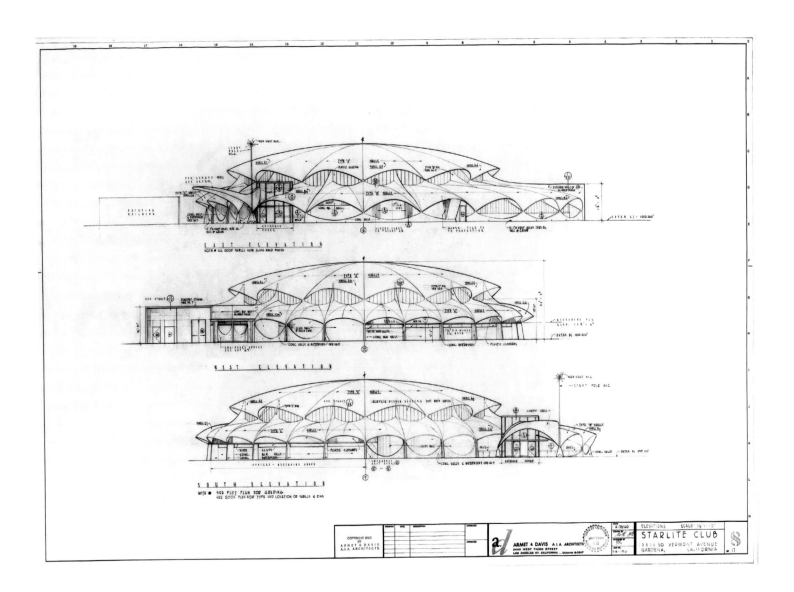

STARLITE CLUB (DIAGRAMS)

The diagrams on this spread delineate the thin-shell concrete building system worked out for this structure, blending the popular appeal of a roadside coffee shop with the size and interior space of a civic building.

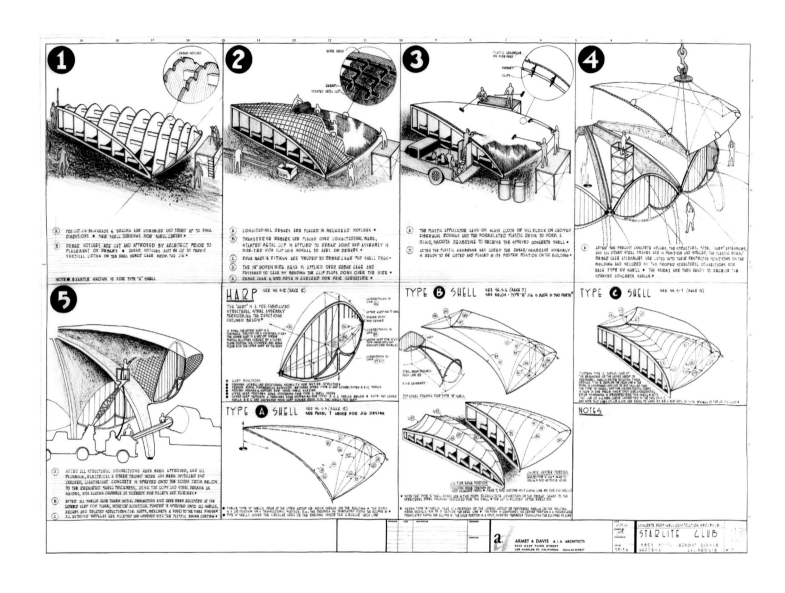

HOT SHOPPES INC.
1961

HOT SHOPPES INC., SCHEME #I
Washington, DC, 1961

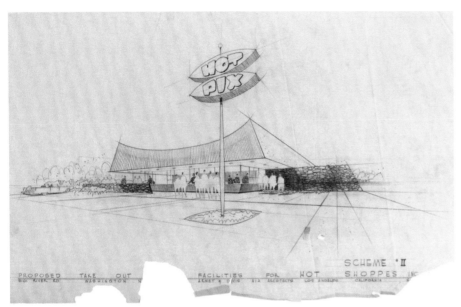

HOT SHOPPES INC., SCHEME #II
Washington, DC, 1961

Eight distinct schemes for Marriott Corporation's proposed Hot Pix fast-food stands, a smaller, walk-up version of its Hot Shoppes restaurants, testify to the formal evolution of the work of Armet & Davis. In them, Googie architecture's fundamental concepts are still evident: a prominent roof performing as the sign, giving a small building presence on the crowded commercial strip; an expression of modern engineering prowess combined with autochthonous natural materials; and convenient parking and outdoor seating, all of which served to keep Modernism popular. From the eight schemes came seven imaginative solutions, four realized in December 1961, followed two months later by three more. Three have tall, sloping roofs, two have flat roofs, and two have low, gabled roofs.

Triangular in plan, Scheme #I, shown at right, boasts structural beams, buttressed by stonework at ground level, that converge and rise into a tall spire. The complementary sign turns the building's motif upside down. A critic may be tempted to see the influence of Eero Saarinen's North Christian Church, in Columbus, Indiana—except the Saarinen building was finished three years later. Customers order at the slanted glass window, an elegant detail unifying the entire design. The pylon rising into the sky is reminiscent of a church spire, but it takes a page from Wayne McAllister's playbook, in this case the Streamline Moderne drive-ins of the 1930s, where tall, central pylons made the small buildings stand out on the bustling strip.

| Client: Marriott Corporation | Rendering by Don Hocker

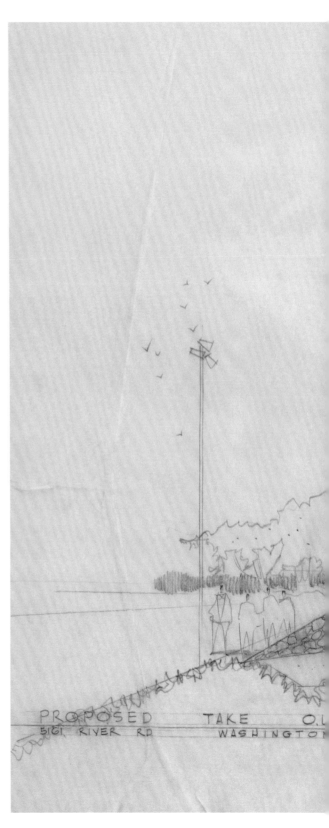

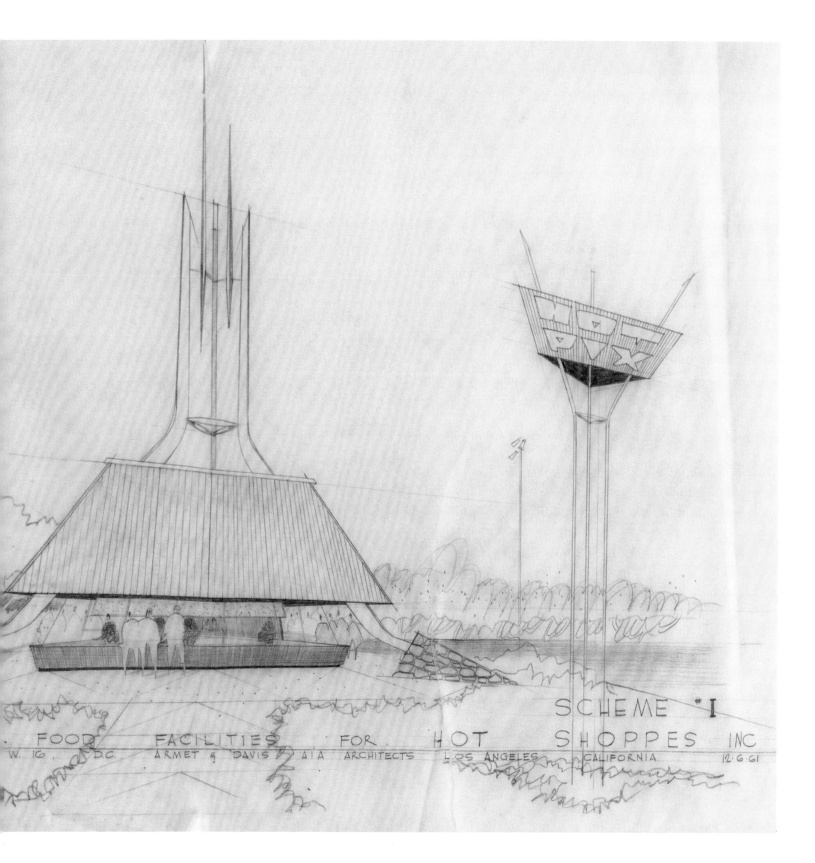

SCHEME #1

FOOD FACILITIES FOR HOT SHOPPES INC

W. 16. D.C. ARMET & DAVIS AIA ARCHITECTS LOS ANGELES CALIFORNIA 12·6·61

SCHEME #III

PROPOSED TAKE OUT FOOD FACILITIES FOR HOT SHOPPES INC.
5161 RIVER RD. — WASHINGTON N.W. 10, D.C.   ARMET & DAVIS AIA ARCHITECTS — LOS ANGELES, CALIFORNIA   12-4-61

HOT SHOPPES INC., SCHEME #III
Washington D.C., 1961

In the rendering above, the sculpted roof rises high on beams braced on stone buttresses. A chevron pattern ornaments its tapered top, while the ends of the structural beams, arranged asymmetrically, burst out at the peak. The design is rooted in Organic architecture in its smoothly sculpted character, geometric ornament, and natural materials—a strong reminder that Googie carries on the American tradition of Modernism, not the European International Style Modernism. The accompanying roadside sign evokes the roof form.
| Client: Marriott Corporation | Rendering by Don Hocker

PROPOSED TAKE O
5161 RIVER RD. — WASHINGTON

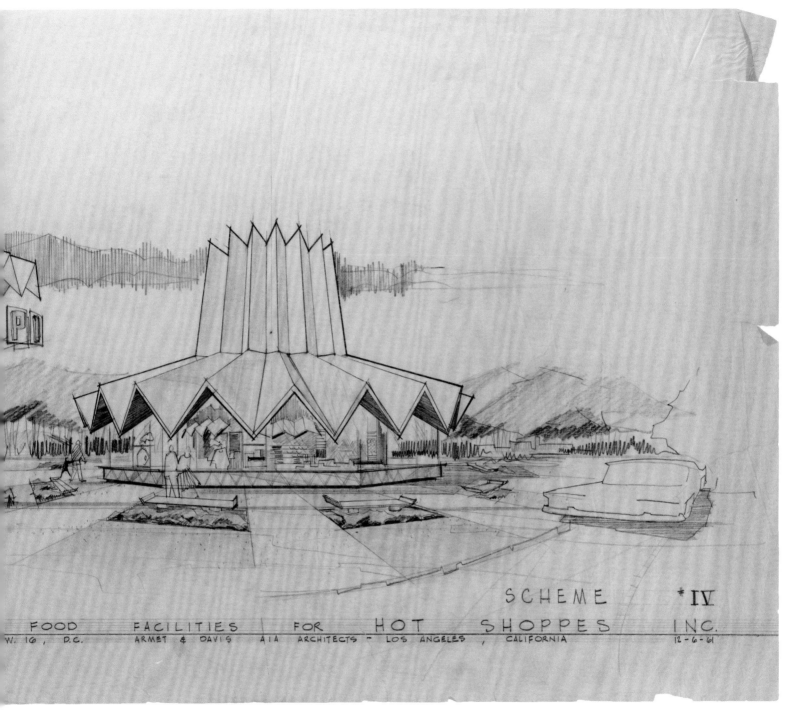

SCHEME #IV

FOOD FACILITIES FOR HOT SHOPPES INC.

W. 16, D.C.   ARMET & DAVIS AIA ARCHITECTS - LOS ANGELES, CALIFORNIA   12-6-61

HOT SHOPPES INC., SCHEME #IV
Washington, DC, 1961

The circular theme of scheme #IV's zigzag folded-plate structure is continued in the radial benches and plantings of the landscape plan. For its part, the inventive freestanding sign deserves dedicated individual study. | *Client: Marriott Corporation* | *Rendering by Don Hocker*

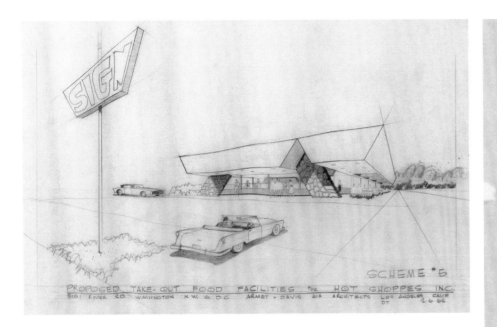

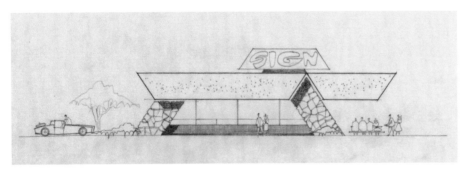

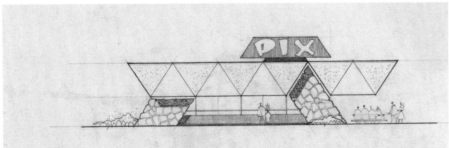

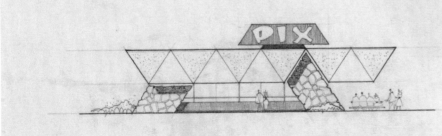

HOT SHOPPES INC., SCHEME #5
Washington, DC, 1962

Scheme #5 (three sketches, top to bottom) is a variation of scheme #11 [page 172], with an extended roof canopy to protect outdoor diners on the right side.
| Client: Marriott Corporation | Rendering by Don Hocker

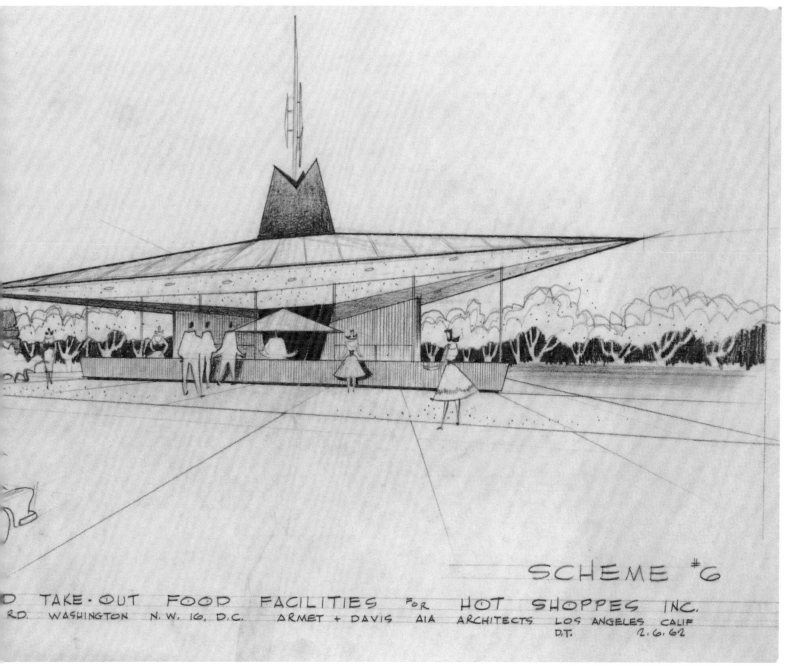

SCHEME #6

D TAKE·OUT FOOD FACILITIES FOR HOT SHOPPES INC.
RD. WASHINGTON N.W. 10, D.C. ARMET + DAVIS AIA ARCHITECTS LOS ANGELES CALIF
D.T. 2.6.62

HOT SHOPPES INC., SCHEME #6
Washington, DC, 1962

Also triangular in plan, scheme #6 (above) focuses its center of gravity at its core. Tapering cantilevers extend to form a crisp edge that hovers over the site, supported entirely from its center. The ceiling slopes down, and interior elements over the kitchen areas echo the roof's attenuated angles. A pylon rises from the center, and a Modern sculpture (compare to Armet & Davis's Chefs Inn design from 1954 [page 57]) rises above that. The entire design is filled with energy and movement—outward to the knife-edge roofline, upward to the pylon and the spear-like sculpture. | *Client: Marriott Corporation | Rendering by Don Hocker*

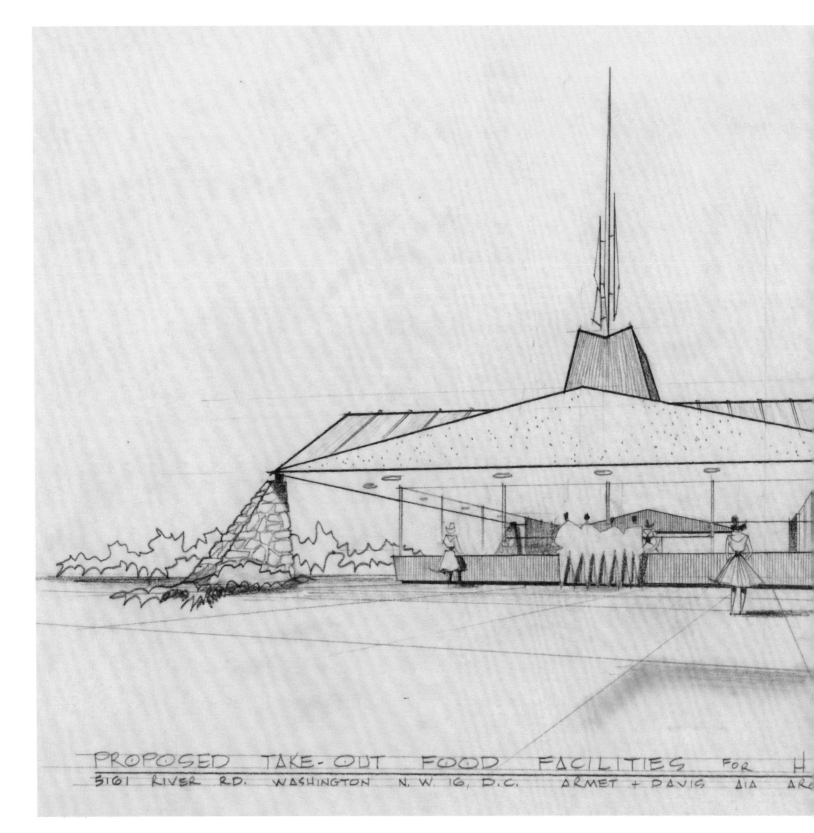

PROPOSED TAKE-OUT FOOD FACILITIES FOR H

5161 RIVER RD. WASHINGTON N. W. 16, D.C.   ARMET + DAVIS AIA ARC

SCHEME #7

SHOPPES INC.

OTS LOS ANGELES CALIF.
D.T. 2.6.62

HOT SHOPPES INC., SCHEME #7
Washington, DC, 1962

In a departure, scheme #7 explores a square plan rather than a triangular one, allowing the roof to be supported delicately on corner stone pylons.

| Client: Marriott Corporation | Rendering by Don Hocker

HOT SHOPPES INC. (OMITTED DESIGN)
Washington, DC, 1962

"Do not send this to Hot Shoppes," reads a note in the lower right corner
of this drawing.
| Client: Marriott Corporation | Rendering by Don Hocker

DID NOT SEND PLAN
TO HOT SHOPPES

PALM SPRINGS SANDS HOTEL
Palm Springs, California, 1961

Two stages of the Palm Springs Sands Hotel show how Googie could apply to larger planning projects such as a resort complex featuring a large convention center. Its Organic Modern architecture could have been a fragment of Frank Lloyd Wright's ideal, decentralized Broadacre City (1934-1958). Though only partially realized, the Sands was envisioned as a major spa hotel and apartments. A later plan included the convention center with a roof suspended by guy wires. At the bottom right of the drawing above, the large entry structure—consisting of two asymmetrical, hexagonal wings topped by decorative finials—shares similarities with Wright's 1958 Gillin House, in Dallas. It is not an imitation but rather a use of Wright's influential Organic design vocabulary. Opposite: views of one of the room wings (top) and the pool terrace (bottom).

| Client: Doran May | Rendering by Vendley | Partially built; extant

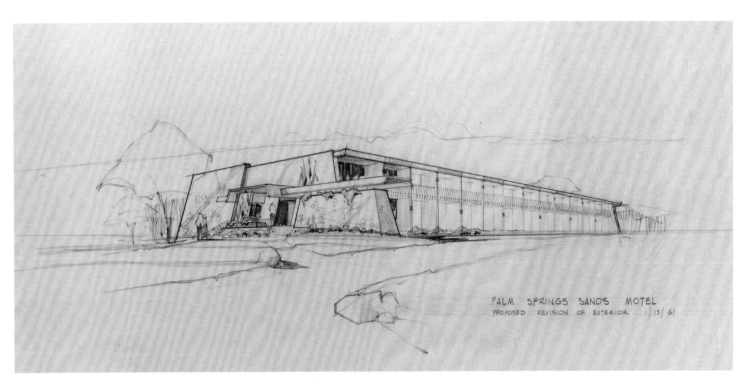

PALM SPRINGS SANDS MOTEL
PROPOSED REVISION OF EXTERIOR 1/15/61

PALM SPRINGS SANDS HOTEL
VIEW FROM EAST LOOKING AT BLDG 'C' AND POOL DECK AREA   BUILDING   SHEET 7
OWNER MR. DORAN MAY   ARMET & DAVIS A.I.A. ARCHITECTS MAR. 14, 1961

Image text within the rendering: 16 Lanes · Coffee Shop · *Starlite* "*Bowl*", RENO

SELDEN AND STEWART, ARCHITECT & PLANNER
ARMET AND DAVIS, ASSOCIATE ARCHITECTS
1041 SOUTH VIRGINIA STREET, RENO

STARLITE BOWL
Reno, Nevada, 1961

| Architect and planner: Selden & Stewart | Associate architects: Armet & Davis | Rendering by Purciel & Nicholl | Built; extant

LYON'S COFFEE SHOP SAN BRUNO, CALIF. LYONS CONCESSIONS

EDWARD WONG

LYON'S COFFEE SHOP
San Bruno, California, 1961

With this prototype for the Lyon's chain, Armet & Davis revisit the prominent prow-like roof of early Huddle schemes [pages 48–49]. By 1961, however, this form, under the architects' eye, had evolved and was now broken up into multiple planes with faceted edges. An outdoor fireplace, shown just right of center in the color rendering above, crowns the street corner as a symbol of welcome. Note the sculptural character of the spear-like sign pylon, whose tapering bottom end points to the fireplace. The roof glides upward from the corner, with slanting planes on either side providing counterpoint and definition. Vestigial beam ends are marked with double racing stripes.
| Associate architect: Edward Wong | Rendering by Alfred W. Gordon | Built; prototype design

ELLIS MOTEL
Calexico, California, 1962

| Client: Sam Ellis | Built; standing

Biff's COFFEE SHOP · OAKLAND   FOR JOSEPH W. DROWN & ROBERT E. COX
ARMET & DAVIS A.I.A. ARCHITECTS

DAVE WILKINS C.A.D.A. '62

BIFF'S COFFEE SHOP
Oakland, California, 1962

A more realistic illustration style is used for one of Armet & Davis's unusual circular designs. Biff's does not rely solely on its eye-catching shape, however; details elaborating the curving shape are seen throughout. The base curves inward, lifting the building visually on diamond-shaped beams. Simultaneously, the stone wall, at left in the above drawing, tethers the structure to the ground. The entry is marked by a sculpted, dropped soffit that directs customers inside. Clamp-like dentils rim the curving roofline, adding to the illusion of a kit of many parts holding the modular pieces of this structure together.
| Client: Joseph W. Drown and Robert E. Cox | Rendering by Dave Wilkins | Built; demolished

WHITE SPOT TAKE-OUT FOOD FACILITIES

WHITE SPOT TAKE-OUT FOOD FACILITIES
Denver, Colorado, 1963

| Client: Bill Clements | Rendering by D.T.

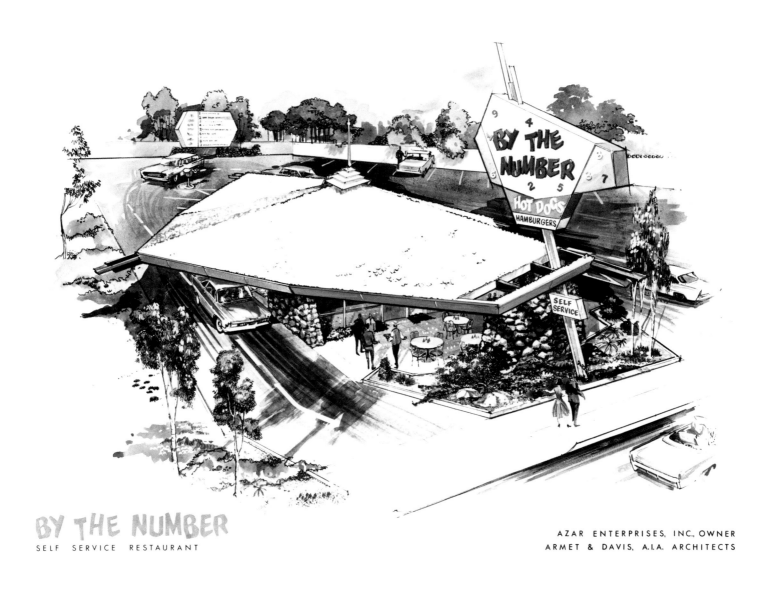

BY THE NUMBER
SELF SERVICE RESTAURANT

AZAR ENTERPRISES, INC., OWNER
ARMET & DAVIS, A.I.A. ARCHITECTS

BY THE NUMBER (PROTOTYPE)
Fort Wayne, Indiana, 1963

In their work for By The Number Self Service Restaurants, Armet & Davis continue to explore the idea of a compact design for a self-service drive-through with outdoor seating, also seen in the firm's concept for the Plush Pup [page 164].
| Client: Azar Enterprises Inc. | Built; demolished

CASINO INTERIOR (UNNAMED)
Las Vegas, c. 1964

This plan for an unidentified casino is a testament to the fact that Googie is a fully three-dimensional architecture capable of shaping complex interior spaces as well as exteriors. The large, open casino floor is articulated spatially by a TV gallery at far left (possibly a sports book for viewing and wagering on sporting events around the country) and Le Carousel at right, an intimate lounge venue under a dropped dome (currently featuring, as drawn, the "L. Prima" band, for singer and bandleader Louis Prima). The umbrellas of the hotel pool terrace can be seen through the windows at center.

KING'S VICTORIA Restaurant

Long Beach Blvd. & Victoria Ave . . . . LONG BEACH

owner: Carson Estate Co.

lessees: Lou Mickey & Jeff King

ARMET & DAVIS AIA
architects ... los angeles

KING'S VICTORIA RESTAURANT
Long Beach, California, 1964

Armet & Davis continued employing the Googie vocabulary of natural stone, wood, and a prominent roofline through the mid-1960s. As public taste began to shift away from sleek, high-tech imagery, especially in California, Googie's exaggerated scale was toned down with more residentially scaled designs such as the one in the above color sketch—the direction in which roadside commercial architecture would be headed.

| Owner: Carson Estate Co. | Client: Lou Mickey and Jeff King | Rendering by Hoey | Built; demolished

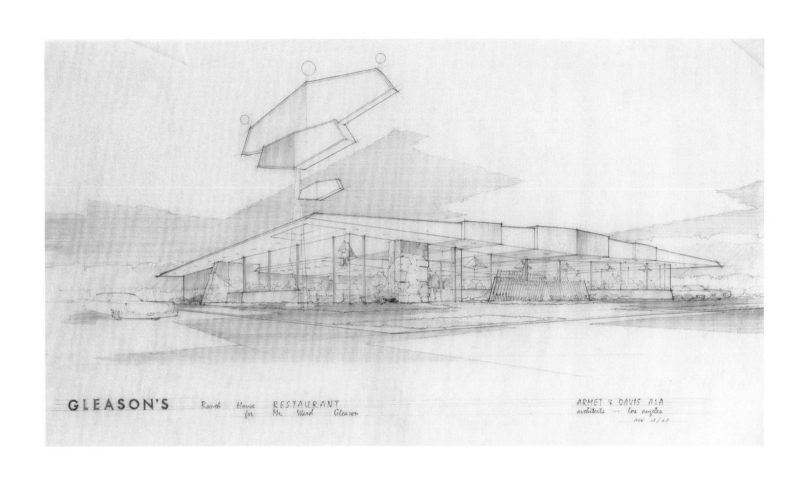

GLEASON'S Ranch House RESTAURANT for Mr. Ward Gleason

ARMET & DAVIS AIA architects ... los angeles Nov. 13/65

GLEASON'S RANCH HOUSE RESTAURANT
Buffalo, New York, 1965

| Client: Ward Gleason

TACO sombrero
albuquerque, n. m.
for: mr. sherman c. anderson.

ARMET & DAVIS AIA
architects ... los angeles

TACO SOMBRERO
Albuquerque, New Mexico, 1965

Car-culture architecture has its roots in appealingly whimsical buildings shaped like giant derbies, oranges, shoes, owls, or dogs, and Armet & Davis would revisit it in their work for Taco Sombrero. As shown above, the building recalls the restaurant's name in an enormous stylized sombrero with a wide, upturned brim and a central crown, artfully abstracted. The motif is carried through in two roadside signs and the light fixtures inside, an example of total design.
| Client: Sherman C. Anderson

PREB'S DRIVE THRU RESTAURANTS ·
FOR MR. RICHARD PREBLE & MR. STAN HESS

ARMET & DAVIS
A·I·A· ARCHITECTS
LOS ANGELES, CALIFORNIA·

PREB'S DRIVE THRU RESTAURANTS
Pasadena, California, 1967

| Client: Richard Preble and Stan Hess

RUSTING SPACESHIPS
/ GOOGIE: TODAY AND ITS FUTURE

By the late 1970s, many coffee shops and bowling alleys were still in business, but decades of wear and layers of badly chosen paint colors had transformed their shiny space-age optimism into rusting spaceships marooned on forgotten planets. They were symbols of a twentieth-century belief that technology held the answers to every problem.

Well, not every problem, as we came to see.

Googie, and Modern architecture in general, was too new to be considered historic, too old to be considered hip. All architectural styles go through this cycle of neglect. Despite the withering criticism it received from establishment schools and historians, and despite multiple demolitions during Googie's decades in the wilderness, enough remained to capture the imagination of future hearts and minds. Googie was, after

all, good architecture—innovative, practical, delightful—that tapped into deep currents in American culture. When a later generation compared it to the calculated blandness of the cookie-cutter commercial buildings and chain restaurant prototypes that were replacing it, or to the stunted, rear-illuminated plastic tombstone signs at shopping centers, the innovative aesthetic and creative practicality of authentic Googie became obvious.

The social and economic value of restoring rather than replacing existing buildings began gaining favor at this time, especially in light of a budding interest in energy sustainability, recycling, and adaptive reuse. My book Googie: Fifties Coffee Shop Architecture (1985) and its follow-up, Googie Redux: Ultramodern Roadside Architecture (2004), brought Googie back into the architectural conversation just as a renewed appreciation for Modern architecture was taking hold. By documenting the buildings and their architects and placing them in the social and design context of their times, both

Johnie's (formerly Romeo's Times Square), 6099 Wilshire Blvd., Los Angeles

books provided historic preservationists with the ammunition to convince landmark commissions, planning commissions, and the public of the importance of and need to conserve this notable chapter of Modernism. Official recognition for these once-overlooked buildings finally came in 1983, when the National Register of Historic Places qualified the oldest McDonald's stand (Stanley Meston, architect, 1953), located in Downey, California. Bob's Big Boy in Burbank (Wayne McAllister, architect, 1949) was named a California Point of Historical Interest in 1993. The Los Angeles Cultural Heritage Commission designated Romeo's Times Square (known today as Johnie's), Norm's La Cienega, and Stanley Burke's (later Corky's)—all designed by Armet & Davis—as Historic-Cultural Monuments. Another Downey restaurant, Harvey's Broiler (Paul Clayton, architect; now a Bob's Big Boy), also qualified for the National Register of Historic Places.

These landmark efforts have been encouraged and supported by preservation organizations such as the Los Angeles Conservancy, but the business community has also seen their value. Harvey's Broiler, the original focal point of Tom Wolfe's dissection of teen style in his essay "The Hair Boys," was restored (after partial demolition) as a Bob's Big Boy with the backing of the city of Downey. Restaurateur Steve Weiss has restored The Penguin in Santa Monica and Kerry's on Ventura Boulevard, both by Armet & Davis, as well as Lane and Schlick's Ben Frank's on the Sunset Strip as part of his Mel's drive-in chain.

Stanley Burke's, built in 1958 on the fabled Van Nuys Boulevard cruising strip, remained in operation as Corky's, though interior remodeling had diminished its architectural character. In 2020, however, a new tenant, Chick-fil-A, also realized Googie's economic potential and, as of this writing, is working to restore the building with the encouragement of the landlord, the family of the original owner. While adaptations will be made to accommodate a drive-through, the character of the original interior, by Helen Fong, will be recaptured, and the new drive-through will creatively continue the spirit of car-culture innovation in Southern California architecture.

A prototype 1964 car wash in Whittier, California, restored in 2018, shows that Googie still plays a practical and even philosophical role in addressing the challenges of the twenty-first century. Clearwater Communities, a developer in Irvine, California, saw the economic advantage of bringing back a profit-generating business while an adjacent, longer-term development was being built on the same property. Clearwater CEO Dan Kassel is also an admirer of the Googie style, the car-culture history it represented, and the public's interest in it.

The restored facility, rechristened Googie Car Wash, successfully exploits a characteristic of historic Googie, that of celebrating modern technology. Clearwater replaced the car wash's original water, chemical, and filtration systems with updated technology that recycles and conserves water (a precious commodity in drought-prone California), and uses safer chemicals, unknown in 1964 but essential today.

Corky's (formerly Stanley Burke's), 5043 Van Nuys Blvd., Sherman Oaks

Simply Wholesome (formerly Wich Stand), 4508 W. Slauson Ave., Los Angeles

A fundamental lesson of historic Googie—that technology can lead to a better life for all—is relevant in the twenty-first century.

Googie teaches the same lesson in relation to the city of today. In the portfolio of Armet & Davis designs featured in this book, original renderings of several coffee shops are superimposed over images of their original locations as they appear in the present day. The sites have changed slowly over the years—so slowly that the cumulative negative impact on the city's public and commercial environment has not been noticed. The contrast of Googie's strong forms—which respond to the strip environment around them—with the boxy, repetitive shapes of the more recent buildings should startle us. Googie, we now know, was intentionally designed by sophisticated architects who understood the urban nature of the new suburban car-culture environment. Those architects exploited its energy and understood its organizational and spatial logic. Critics who labeled Southern California's Googie landscape "unplanned sprawl" were badly misinformed.

Googie was once the future. Does it have a future today? Ironically, Armet & Davis's Tiny Naylor's restaurant, a notable car-culture monument on La Cienega near Wilshire, fell to the wrecking ball, clearing the way for construction of the Wilshire subway line, the next chapter in Los Angeles's transportation history. Uber, Lyft, and autonomous vehicles are ushering in what architect-planner Denise Scott Brown calls the "car-option society." Will that society respond with the same inventiveness and imagination that Googie did when it emerged from the first generation of the car culture?

VICTOR NEWLOVE
/ INTERVIEW

Victor Newlove, a native of Culver City who was raised in both San Jose and Santa Monica, California, began working for Armet & Davis as a summer intern before graduating from Notre Dame University's School of Architecture in 1964. He worked with architects Thornton Abell and Jones & Emmons prior to returning to Armet & Davis as a partner in 1972. What follows is an edited compilation of conversations between Victor Newlove, Alan Hess, and Michael Murphy recorded on April 17, 2021, and June 7, 2021, at the Armet Davis Newlove offices in Santa Monica, where Newlove still practices.

Q: There's so much to talk about how the office worked, how design decisions were made, who was on the staff, what clients thought, and architectural questions about details, planning, and intentions, as well as how the drawings were created. Let's just start.

VN: The first design, of course, for a coffee shop client was for Forest Smith, the guy who did Clock restaurants. If you take a look at it, the Clock design is unique [36-37].

Q: With the triangular windows?

VN: I think it's a pretty good one.

Q: Smith was a frequent early client. Armet & Davis also designed Clock Country Club for him. Paul S. Cummins was also a frequent client, with the Huddle restaurants. How did Norm Roybark come to Armet & Davis?

VN: The story goes that Roybark is at the racetrack. In those days, a lot of people used to go to the track. Horse racing was a big deal. Tiny Naylor used to lose a lot of money at the track, and the story was, Roybark asked, "How can you afford to lose money like this?" And Naylor replied, "Well, it's because I have these restaurants, you know, the Tiny Naylor's restaurants, and we use Armet & Davis as the architect." That's how Norm Roybark got us. Norm was a car salesman and basically liked the idea of having a restaurant, which was almost a car showroom.

Q: How did Eldon Davis and Louis Armet divide up work, or how did they work together?

VN: They didn't really work together, but basically they had separate work, separate clients. I would say that Eldon was the primary architect and designer rather than Louis. Louis Armet was a nice guy. He did most of the religious architecture.

Q: Did Armet have connections to the archdiocese?

VN: Probably. He was Catholic. He did do some restaurants, but only Eldon did most restaurants. So [Louis] took over what I would consider the ones that were minor clients. Most of the major restaurant clients were Eldon's and Helen Fong's.

Q: Tell me about Helen. How did she work?

VN: Well, first off, she came from Eugene Choy's office.

Q: Within the same building, right?

VN: Yes and no. At one time they had buildings across the street from each other. They were always close, Eldon and Eugene. That was in the early 1950s. Then Helen went to work full time for Eldon Davis.

Q: How would you describe Helen and Eldon's working relationship? It seems that Eldon really respected and relied on her on these different design projects. We saw that when one of Helen's interiors, badly remodeled, was uncovered for a restoration. Her original design, materials, and lighting were far superior.

VN: She was the interior designer, and she was the person who really stepped up to make the interiors the way they were. She was a detail-oriented person. She influenced greatly the interiors of these restaurants. A lot of architects used to consider the exteriors to be "roofatecture." You come up with these bizarre designs, or these far-out designs, or these great designs in my particular opinion, where you combine the signage and the landscaping and everything all together.

But the interiors! How do you do the colors? How do you pick out the furniture that's going to go in there? How are you going to make it interesting inside? A lot of architects don't have the ability to do that, but Helen did. So yeah, she was a really good interior designer.

Q: This book is full of drawings—how did you use these drawings?

VN: First thing you do is you have a meeting with a client and discuss what kind of design you want. We would come up with some design sketches, and the client would say yea or nay, or that he wanted something completely different. We have a drawing of an elevation of Norm's, as an example. That was what the final design really kind of looked like. Those rough sketches [pages 68-71] were actually in between the design development drawings, versus something that you would then hand over to the drafting team of the company. Then they would provide the working drawings.

Q: How would those preliminary sketches have been used in the process?

VN: The sketches Lee Linton did, I almost considered them set designs for a movie. I mean, they're concept sketches. To get the building to look like that, you couldn't build his buildings like that. You could come close, but he would do a great concept sketch. And then you would work from that point to try to make something that would fit on this particular piece of property. He had one where they had the barrel vault for Carolina Pines, as an example, which did get built on Vermont Avenue [page 83]. In that particular case, you were supposed to represent concrete vaults. Well, it didn't get built out of concrete. It was built out of plaster. You could build it out of concrete, [but] you couldn't afford it. A lot of our buildings are never meant to last a hundred years. Twenty years, thirty, tops.

Q: There are a lot of Linton's really jazzy drawings. What was the purpose of those? Was that to sell it to the client, to get them excited about it?

VN: Yeah, exactly. We knew what we wanted in those days. I mean, I'm speaking for Lee Linton without ever having known the man. All I know is his drawings. He was just a flamboyant designer, and he was a damn good designer, but he would be a good set designer, concept designer. You can tell his figures, the figures are what gives it up. This one [Googies, page 92-93] isn't by Linton—too stiff.

Q: But Linton's drawings drew you in, almost like a movie. In a two-dimensional drawing, you have both the wide shot and then the close-up as you walk in and see the people sitting at the counter. So it is very cinematic.

VN: Right. That's why he was successful working in Vegas.

Q: Did Helen ever do the interior renderings?

VN: Never. I don't think she could. She would direct people to do it. When I did the Denny's [Prototype #2, page 119], she pretty much directed me as to what she wanted for the interiors and exteriors. And my exterior sketches were completely different from my interior sketches.

Q: Really? Why?

VN: You know, I don't know why. It's easy for me to do an exterior sketch because I can fake it a lot. But you can't do that with an interior sketch. It had to have been fairly accurate. And there lies the problem, because you can't hide it with a goddamn tree. Planting and trees, cars, people, things like that. You couldn't do that for the interior.

Q: What kind of suggestions would she give when you were working on an interior?

VN: Well, we would discuss... I'll just take the Denny's [Prototype #2]. There we wanted a car theme on the inside, so we had the car seats for the booth work like an automobile seat. And I remember doing those and designing them.

Q: You mean like the pleating on the—

VN: Yeah, the pleating on the car seats. Just like the car. We were going to make it like a damn car. It's the car culture, for God's sake. Then the other thing was that I wanted to take the canopies and everything inside to reflect what was done on the outside.

Then I used wild colors on the inside, because again, we didn't want anybody to fall asleep in the restaurant. I had started work with another architect, prior to Armet & Davis, that introduced me to marking pens. Marking pens were a really new thing in 1962. Nobody had them.

But I worked for a company called Medical Planning Associates, and they introduced me to the basic marking pens, Magic Markers. Boy, from that point on that changed my entire life, just to find those marking pens, and I learned how to draw with those. Then when I went back to college, I used [them] and everybody was amazed at the colors I was able to achieve. I said, "Well, this is something new."

You were limited then to the colors of the Magic Markers. So for the Denny's, what we wanted was to use really bright colors on the interior. You have a limited palette. But I had ways of toning them down and toning them up only because if you practice enough times, you learn how to use what you've got. The idea was to use a lot of color to make the interior not boring. We wanted punch. Or, if you were like people who worked at Norm's, the idea was to get them in and get them out. He'd put a timer on the goddamn table that'll tell you you had so much time to eat.

Q: You mean Norm Roybark himself?

VN: Not Roybark himself. I'm talking about Sterling Bogart, who was his successor. His feeling was that we just don't want people to stay there for any great length of time. Bright colors. We don't want them to be relaxed and [bored] and fall asleep inside the restaurant. I mean, that was his idea.

VN: I still make sketches. I use Magic Markers with other, mixed media in order to achieve what I want. Because I'll use correction tape, Wite-Out. I'll use pencils and colored pencils and that sort of thing. I'll use anything to make something look like what I want. That's how we would do an interior. The idea was to use a lot of color to make the interior not boring.

Q: You mentioned the renderers. My impression is that there are a lot of drawings from the '50s that are recognizably by Lee Linton. But then some of the later ones, like the circular Biff's up in Oakland, look like those of a professional renderer.

VN: They were professional renderers. I'm trying to remember the artists. We used to hire renderers.

Q: Linton was definitely a renderer and an architect, for all intents and purposes, and really designing the concept of the building in these drawings. But then, after that, into the 1960s and '70s, there seem to be more professionally done renderings for the clients.

VN: Yeah. The concept drawings would be done by Lee or myself or Don Hocker. Then we would get a professional renderer to come in to do it. We had a whole bunch of these people.

Q: Was there a reason for that?

VN: Yeah, it's more finished and it looks better. It's more of a realistic presentation too.

We depended on outside sources for everything, if we could do it. We never had in-house electrical, mechanical, structural. We hired outside people. We hired outside artists to do renderings for us. We hired artists to do murals. We hired certain people that specialized in chandeliers and lighting.

Q: You have mentioned that you sat behind Kaz Nomura at Jones & Emmons. As I've been studying all these things, I think that Linton was just as good. I mean, a different style, but boy, he captured so much in those drawings.

VN: I loved watching some people really draw. That's why Don Hocker was so great.

Q: When did you first start working for Armet & Davis?

VN: I was a student at college. I went to Notre Dame, and I would come home every summer and try to get a job in architecture. First company I ever worked for was Medical Planning Associates. I was an office boy, basically. But it was my first experience working in an office. They discovered that I could draw, and I was doing some designs for them at that time.

I ended up coming home the next summer, and I needed a job. And I walked into Glenn Lundberg's office over on San Vicente because I was living over in West L.A. and I said, "I'm looking for a job." And I looked around and there was nobody else in the office, just Lundberg. He says no, but he arranges for me to go over to see Eldon Davis the next day at their office over on West Third Street. So I went over there and I showed him my portfolio, if you could call it that, and told him that I needed a job and all happy stuff like that. Finally I got impatient and I said, "Well, are you going to hire me? Or what am I doing here?" He said, "We'll hire you, you can start the next day. You can start right now, actually." So there are thirty-five people in the drafting room. I didn't know anything about Armet & Davis at all. Except that I knew about the Huddles, and I knew about Norm's. I knew about Bob's Big Boy, because they were all

my favorite restaurants. I mean, this is crazy. I knew about it. But I didn't go in there because of that. I didn't know who the hell these guys were.

So that's how I got hired. And that's how I met Helen Fong. Then I realized who the real boss was: Helen Fong.

Q: What do you mean by that?

VN: She was the boss of the drafting room. I mean, let's face it. I was a damn draftsman. I was like a slave. I was there mainly to gain experience. I was there to learn; this was my graduate school.

Q: What was her interest or sensibility? What was she like as a personality working with people?

VN: Well, she was tough. She was a tough person to get along with sometimes. She taught me to love opera and classical music. Good businesswoman.

[After I started working,] they said, "What are you going to do when you get out of college? Would you like to come to work for us permanently?" And I said yeah. I didn't take any time off. I didn't believe in taking time off.

I was also working for other architects. I worked for a guy by the name of Burnette Turner. He was a fellow in the American Institute of Architects. We did renovation work for Olvera Street. So we did the Pico House, the Garnier Building, the church, and the substation for the trollies. These were some of the oldest structures in Los Angeles. Our job was to stabilize these buildings and convert them to other uses without tearing them down.

Then I wanted to learn how to do houses and things like that, and so I went to work, the same time I was working for Armet & Davis, for Thornton Abell doing drafting for him doing houses. I was freelancing as usual.

Q: What kinds of projects?

VN: College work, laboratories. Though the one I still have the drawing for is a house that was done in Palos Verdes Estates.

Q: Abell had a highly regarded reputation.

VN: Oh, very good architect, yeah. I learned a lot of how...how do I say it? He was thorough. Interviewing his clients and knowing what they wanted. He had a specific style of architecture that he really wanted to produce. This particular house [in Palos Verdes] was for a USC professor who liked plants, so they had a lot of greenhouses, that sort of thing. And Thornton loved plants. He and his wife loved to grow plants. Irises. That was their big deal.

Then I decided that I would like to work, really, for [A.] Quincy Jones. I had been interviewed to work for him. But in the meantime I had accepted the job already to leave Armet & Davis and work for Thornton Abell. And at the same time that Thornton hired me, Jones called me up and said, "I'd like to hire you," and I said, "I can't, I've accepted another job with Thornton Abell. Even though I want to work for you, I am obligated to work for him."

They all knew each other, they were all good friends. But I said [to Jones] I would like to eventually work for you. So I worked for Thornton Abell and then he kind of ran out of work and he called Jones. He knew I always wanted to work for Jones.

Q: Why?

VN: Quincy Jones was one of the best architects in Los Angeles. I had the interview with him. So all of a sudden, I found myself over at Jones & Emmons. I learned more from Jones's office, in particular from Kaz Nomura, one of the finest draftsman designers I had ever seen.

Kaz established the style of all of the renderings that came out of that office, absolutely. And I worked right behind him and watched him work. Then we would do presentations, and he would tell me what to do presentation-wise. I would follow him. And I copied him, to be honest with you. I learned from this man. It was like, hell, I should have paid them to work for them. I captured his style of rendering.

Q: What kind of buildings did you work on at Jones & Emmons?

VN: Mostly university work. Some fairly major buildings at UCLA, University of California Santa Barbara, UC San Diego, and UC Irvine. I had nothing to do with making any decisions. I would do presentation drawings, that sort of thing. I worked on the Eichler houses and all that too.

Q: So you met Joe Eichler also?

VN: Kaz was in charge of the Eichler houses. I was working with Kaz. Mr. Eichler would come into the office and have meetings with us and talk about the details, how the houses were to go together, the design concepts, and everything else. That was the only client I was even allowed to talk to. Mr. Eichler was, how do I say it? You could actually talk to the guy, which was terrific. Yeah, he was just a nice man. I learned a lot from the guy.

Q: Because he seemed to be really involved with the details.

VN: Right down to the details, absolutely. How things look, yes. He wanted it this way, this way, and we would draw it for him. Who was I to tell him no? But I wasn't ever going to do that anyway.

Q: What did you learn then from [Jones & Emmons]?

VN: Discipline, and what it was like to be an architect. I mean, I got my license there in 1968. I was twenty-six or twenty-seven years old, and I got a license, which is pretty young. But then I was doing my own work on the side about that time. So I worked for Jones for about a year and a half, two years, three.

Q: And then you came back to Armet & Davis.

VN: I was always working for Armet & Davis—I never stopped working for Armet & Davis. I saw them all the time. Jones didn't like the fact. You're not supposed to work for other architects. Jones kind of looked down on Armet & Davis—very much so.

Q: Tell us about that.

VN: They were snobs. I would never admit that I did the Bob's Big Boy design—and it was mine. I never admitted it. I never admitted the fact that I did the Denny's design—I was almost embarrassed. They were being built all over the country. But I just never told them that I did it. I mean, I wasn't proud of it, because it wasn't a purist-type architecture like Jones and Thornton Abell did. I mean, these guys were [from] the school of Neutra, Schindler, and really good architects, but we were never considered "good" architects.

We'd built basically for the masses, and they weren't necessarily buildings that had great architectural integrity. Yet they did have architectural integrity. They had a theory behind everything that they did [at Armet and Davis].

Q: In what way?

VN: We believed that the outside and inside should integrate. The landscaping should just blend into the inside. You should be able to look through the inside and not have any barriers. The building floats, has a lot of glass, you can see a lot of that animation and color inside, and lighting. All of this really was the way [Armet & Davis] did their drawings. It was their concepts.

It was a system that they used over and over again, an analysis. Their design concepts were to keep things open and clear—animation, color, lights—and then integrate the signs, integrate the materials, try to come up with new materials all the time. Use materials that, as an example, Jones & Emmons would never use—stone, wood, concrete, and everything, together. They would never do that. We basically wanted to have walls which spoke to you of different materials, so that when you looked in a building, things changed. You weren't bored to death in your buildings.

But I learned a lot from some of these architects. In particular, Thornton, and how he used concrete. He used concrete like it was the real material, not making it smooth. He would use board forms on the concrete to make it look like it had boards. It had a feeling to it.

[Armet & Davis] had the same concept. They wanted things to be open,

Armet & Davis commissioned many fine artists to design custom artwork for their coffee shops that included stained glass, light fixtures, decorative screens, door pulls, and murals. This maquette (below), for a mural inside a Carolina Pines Jr., showing stylized birds, some perched on branches, is by the wife-and-husband team of Betsy Hancock and Hans Werner.

[so they] used a lot of glass too. So both of those architects actually did use the same concepts that Armet & Davis were using, but in a different way. They had better materials. They had richer clients. They had the universities or the government [as clients].

Q: Agree completely. That sense of openness and the glass walls—in the Case Study Houses and A. Quincy Jones houses. They would have those glass walls looking out to the view or the garden. You were doing commercial buildings. You turned that glass wall to the street. That was the whole purpose.

VN: We wanted to be able to look in. We want to be able to look out too. Look, when you're in the restaurant, there are two things you're going to look at. You're going to look out on the street and look at the animation of the trucks and cars and everything that's going by. The other thing was, you're looking at the animation of the cooking lines and seeing what was going on inside. So there was a concept.

Q: Yeah. That's the function of the building, to serve the customers. That's how you designed it then, so that they would be pleased.

VN: Like I mentioned, it's a damn food factory.

Q: You returned to Armet & Davis so you could continue your own design work.

VN: I was not just designing. I was doing the work once I got my license. I had buildings under construction, under my own name. And I had people who would hire me, which is really strange—but they did. I did a lot of additions for a lot of people in Brentwood and that area. A lot of additions to houses. One recommended me, and then everybody kept recommending me. Finally, I got so much work, I couldn't stay [at Jones & Emmons] any longer.

I even had a General Telephone Credit Union building I was doing in Santa Monica. It was my own work. What are you going to do? So I had to leave. I went to work for Armet & Davis at the time because they would let me do my work on the side. Jones & Emmons never let me do that.

I finally told Eldon, "Look, I've got to leave. I have an office that I already arranged for with Burnette Turner, Sandy Turner." I was going to rent a space from him as a draftsman in his office. So [Eldon and Louis] said, "Well, listen, we'll make you a partner."

And I said, "Wow." Then I thought about it: Well, you know, it's not too bad if you're a partner in the firm. Maybe I'll last a couple of weeks or a month. Then they decided to even change the name of the firm at the time, and that was in '72.

I remember when I first became partner in the firm. They handed me all of the bills that were unpaid, or the invoices. [Helen] said, "See if you can collect." I almost cried when I looked at them. In those days, we had $300,000 worth of receivables. I thought, They don't even know how to collect money. Where are the contracts? No contracts—no nothing. Everything was a handshake, and that's bullshit. You've got to document things. Some of our clients were not paying, and collecting money was always a...we were always on the verge of [being] broke. I mean the 1980s, I remember there was no money, no way to survive, but we always did. We always found new work. Everybody else, all their other offices quit, gone.

Q: Tell us about Denny's.

VN: Here's a story of Denny's. We did the original Denny's [page 68-77], which were called Danny's. OK? This is before I ever got there. Basically [Denny's founder] Harold Butler got a phone call from an attorney saying, "You can't use the Danny's." Like it was Coffee Dan's. "Or I'm going to sue you. Do not use Danny's anymore." So what are you going to do? You change the A to an E and call it Denny's. Cheaper.

That was his solution. So then from that point on, because we had a lot of designs in the flat file where they were Danny's, we started doing Denny's. We had been doing Norm's [page 114]. I think that was the first time Norm's fired Armet & Davis, because we started doing work for Denny's. Norm felt the design was a little too close to Norm's—which it was. But we did, like, three or four hundred Denny's and we didn't do that many Norm's. Hell, they never had very many restaurants. That was the first of three or four times that we were fired by them. I was fired at least twice.

Q: But then you would go back to work for them.

VN: Yeah. I would get these phone calls. They would hire some architect, and the guy would just butcher some job, and then they would say, "You want to come back and work for us?" I was like, yeah. I would do about three restaurants, and then they'd fire me again. They'd get pissed off at me because the jobs were too expensive, I don't know what. One time I got fired—I know—because my fees were too high.

Q: Talking about the clients, was there a particular client that you did interact with a lot that you can talk about?

VN: Yeah. Well, actually, I did work for Bob Wian [of Bob's Big Boy]. It was interesting because I was just out of college and I was doing a design for the new Bob's theme.

Bob Wian was a friend of [Clock client] Forest Smith, and they went to high school together. That's the reason why Bob Wian came to Armet & Davis. How Eldon knew Forest Smith, I don't know. [Armet & Davis's] first Bob's design was a curved roof with stone-supporting columns [page 126]. This was built five or six times. That was the only one that was really a Googie style.

The next phase of design, which started in 1965, was the ranch-house thing, the Chula Vista building, which we did [page 149]. First built in Chula Vista. We were getting away from the old style of real bright colors. We wanted the muted tones in those days because that's what was selling. All we cared about is, how do you make the client a success? That was the deal. How can you sell hamburgers? What will people like to see and do?

Q: But did that change over time?

VN: Sure. Of course it did. The designs became more muted and relaxed and more dinner-house style here in California. But the California coffee shop designs were still prevalent back east because they were about twenty years behind. So we were selling one brand of architecture back east and one brand here in California.

Q: It's total design. Everything goes together. The colors, the shapes, the artwork, the exterior and interior and all. California was always in advance.

VN: We were so far in advance. These designs then became passé, which is unfortunate. But that's the way it was.

Q: Tell me more about Bob Wian. Who was he? What kind of person was he? What was he interested in?

VN: Really nice individual. I worked with Wian directly. I was shocked that Eldon would even consider that. I would come up with the sketches. I'd take them over, and he would look at them. [Wian] wanted a ranch-style restaurant, a new design that really went away from the Googie-style architecture, in that particular case. So he had a floor plan which he already had and he liked, by another architect, but basically we were to take the other architect's floor plan, change it, and then come up with a new design. So I worked on that particular one with Mr. Wian and Eldon, and we came up with the design that almost looked like a residential-style architecture.

But it still had the concept of openness and exposed structure and the use of natural woods, cork ceilings. The raised planters brought the landscaping almost into the room at eye level. All of the air-conditioning was underground; I didn't want to have drop ceilings. We did have some in the kitchens, obviously, things like that. But in the main dining room, we didn't work with them. Wian approved the exterior design, and then we would work on the interior design with Helen, and she would come up with the colors and the concepts. We would try to figure out what we were going to do. I think the stained glass was Helen's idea, on the ends. I don't know if I really liked the idea of the stained glass.

The reason why the stained glass was there was that [because] you couldn't put the shades down, you put [in] the stained glass so the sun wouldn't come in. And it also gave a lot of color at nighttime. You have it backlit.

We would sit there and design the light fixtures, and I used to design the light fixtures and figure out where the signage was going to go and what type of a booth we were going to end up having. We would work with Helen on that. Lighting, of course, is an extremely important part of our restaurants and the interiors to get the animation, to be able to look through the glass and to be able to see what's going on. But you had to make it interesting to look through a building and see the lighting. Again, you're looking at something that is, and I've mentioned this before, it's almost like an automobile showroom where you look [in] and instead of being an automobile on sale, it's food, people.

Q: What sorts of things were you looking at for the lighting?

VN: In my particular case, I was always looking to see how bright I could make it and to be able to emphasize certain areas, like walls. Like, if you had something on a wall, how are you going to light that? And you want to be able to concentrate your light. Do you want to light a counter? You light the counter specifically every once in a while over the counter to make sure the counter was well lit. You had lighting, general illumination inside. But you didn't want to make it look like an office. You wanted to make it look like you can see high and low points of the architecture inside.

A lot of times, we would have the pie cases lit brightly where you're trying to sell the pies. You're selling the pies, but it's also a light source inside the building at the same time. And you're doing exhibition cooking, which they had in this particular place, the exhibition cooking is going to be well lit. So you wanted to light the cooking area not only because it's better for the cooks to cook but [also] to be able to see the animation from inside and outside. So you want to emphasize, This is the show. It's a show. It's a damn theatrical show.

Q: How did you light the ceiling? Where is that light coming from?

VN: Well, the lights are all recessed lighting. Then you would also have those lights that are hanging down. Those were meant to kind of break up the lighting. Those would be the George Nelson-type lights. In fact,

they used George Nelson a lot. They used Herman Miller furniture, as an example. They used nothing but the best. So [Helen] was very conscious, and we were always conscious of lighting. We always did our own lighting. I mean, I did my lighting, she did hers. We tried to use the latest technology that we could to be able to really brighten the places up.

Q: What kind of decisions did Helen make?

VN: Well, it was collaborative. I mean, you say decisions, you didn't really make decisions. You sat around and said, "We got to do this, we got to do that." It was a collaborative type of thing. In that particular case, it was myself and Helen. Once we got through the exterior, Eldon kind of walked away from the project, kind of left it up to me, which was crazy. I mean, I was just a young kid, so it was interesting. And this was before I even had a license, for God's sake. I was just out of college. But I was acting as their designer. Also did Denny's [Prototype #2, page 119] about that time too, come to think of it—the Denny's [design that] got built, like, seventy times.

That was one of the last things I did before I left and then went to work for Thornton Abell and then later to Quincy Jones.

Q: Tell us about the landscaping.

VN: As far as landscaping, Sid Galper was our main landscape man. Sid I knew for years and years. Galper-Baldwin was the name. He was absolutely the guy that we went to from the beginning of the 1950s until he finally ended up dying. Then we used some of his people later that came from his office as well.

Sid had an ability to do landscaping that you could carry through from inside to outside. We would take trees through the roof and all that kind of thing, holes through the roof. They would take the lighting, as an example, and bury the lighting so you couldn't see the light source. You'd bury the lighting in underground cylinders so you'd have uplighting on the columns. But the landscaping was an integral part of the design. No doubt about it.

Q: OK, so you've mentioned these elements: the lighting, the architecture, the landscaping. Take any example. How would the team have worked to get that blending?

VN: Well, first off, you came up with a concept sketch of what it was going to be: the exterior and what the building was going to be before you came up with a floor plan. Again, you're looking at a food factory. Got to be able to produce food, so you've got to have a plan that is very efficient, and boy, they knew how to do plans. They knew how to do food service.

We would start a lot of times with the food service equipment designers, Stan Abrams, Abrams & Tanaka. Great food service equipment designers, along with others. So you would start with a plan and get the design for the food service and start with the menu first. Find out what you were going to be serving and do an efficient plan, do the exterior design to go with the plan, and try to site it to a particular site.

Then it was a matter of doing the working drawings and figuring out all the things we talked about before: the lighting, and what we were going to do in the inside. What are we going to do to make it unique? I think the Huddle restaurants were some of the best interiors that I've ever seen. I say that because I remember going to the Huddle in Santa Monica [page 48]. I was a kid, and I was impressed at the time with the Huddle, and I knew that it was a special restaurant. I could sense it—and

I was just a little kid. I didn't know Armet & Davis. Didn't know who they were at all. The one at the Santa Monica Airport was, I think, one of the best they ever did.

Q: Why do you think it was the best one?

VN: Unique in colors, the fact that it changed levels, had a view of the airport. You can't do it today. It was a funny, great building, a very entertaining building to be in. And you would look at the use of stained-glass murals, artwork. I don't think I'd ever seen anything quite like that in a building before. It was one of the best. The other one that was really, really good, of course, was Wich Stand, which I think was a really, really fine design, the whole theme, all the way through the building.

Q: It seems like Frisch's and Blazo's and the other Big Boy franchises back east didn't use the same design that Bob Wian was using out here. They had their own designs.

VN: Yeah. We would come up with our own designs. They all wanted something different, and therefore plans were always different. There were different menus sometimes too.

Q: How did the evolution of the restaurant industry affect the work in the Armet & Davis office? In the 1950s, it looks like there were a lot of individual restaurants, a few at a time, like Norm's. But then sometime around 1960, chains like Denny's and Bob's started to—

VN: They started changing the design concepts away from the movie-style architecture. There was probably another factor going on too. Things were changing as we saw it.

Eventually in Southern California [for] the coffee shops—except for Denny's, which would go out all over the country—land was starting to get pretty expensive. It was economics. I think the advent of McDonald's and the concept of fast-food restaurants tried to eat away at the restaurant industry. The style of architecture changed. You always had to keep abreast of what the style of architecture was.

Q: The Hot Shoppes drawings [page 172-180], is that part of that story?

VN: Yeah, it is. We worked with Marriott for years. Eldon started with them, and we used to have meetings with Dick Marriott, who was the head of that particular division. We'd always meet [in Scottsdale, Arizona]. In the wintertime, they'd always come out here because it was too cold back there.

Q: [The Hot Shoppes] are seven individual little drawings. They're small, they were like McDonald's service.

VN: Yeah, for fast food.

Q: But they were gorgeous. Did they build those?

VN: They built a bunch of Hot Shoppes, sure.

Q: These are just extraordinary. Do you know who drew those? Or designed those?

VN: Don Hocker.

Q: Who were some of the other main people, designers and architects, in Armet & Davis's office in the '50s, before you were there?

VN: Lee Linton. He was there just prior to me being there. They were looking to replace a designer at the time, and that's really basically how I came [on]—they figured I had some talent as a designer. But nothing like this guy. This guy was really a good craftsman and a good artist.

Don Hocker worked here at the office. He was their chief designer

when I came in. He was the guy that did these [Hot Shoppes] renderings and sketches [pages 166-175].

Q: They're really beautiful.

VN: Oh, yeah. He was a great artist. What year do you think these are from? I loved Don Hocker, he was the nicest guy in the world. He went to Carnegie Tech, and that's all I can tell you. He was from Johnstown, Pennsylvania. Then we had Caldwell and Ray in here. What happened was that basically Caldwell and Ray left the firm to form their own firm, but they stole the Denny's [business] from us. That was a big deal.

Q: That was a huge account.

VN: Yeah. So my design was to counter their design because we had a smaller building, and we offered that building then as a completely different design from the [previous] Denny's [prototype]. [Harold] Butler actually liked the design.

Q: Which design was that?

VN: That was the one I did for the [Denny's Prototype #2, page 113]. I never quite liked it. You try to avoid certain sections of town because of the buildings you did. It's terrible, but that's the way it goes. But you know what? You do so many buildings, some of them are actually hits. You understand what I'm saying? It's just you've done so many buildings, some are good, some are bad. You know what I mean? Hey, that's the forces of life. Not all the buildings I did were that great. But most of them were, thank God. That's the reason why we're still in business here.

Q: What's your favorite building that you did?

VN: I think some of the churches, because they actually took the concepts of the restaurants. I think the best one I ever did was Saint Kateri Tekakwitha [2007, Santa Clarita, California], which seats 1,400 people. It's all glass walls.

Q: What about additions to the Bob's Big Boy in Burbank?

VN: Well, I did that, I think in the '70s. I was doing all of the Bob's at the time. They wanted to remodel that one by Wayne McAllister. So I looked at the building and thought, I have the drawings. So I doubled the size of the dining room and kept the same design. We also renovated the sign because it was falling apart, so we restored the neon. Everything had to be redone.

Q: Armet & Davis worked with a lot with people, like Hans Werner and Betsy Hancock, who were well-respected artists, and with many other freelance artists and craftspeople who did custom-designed murals, screens, door pulls, light sconces, chandeliers.

VN: We're brokers. I'm a broker, an architect. I bring people together to put a project together. That's what we did. We had disciplines that we used over and over again. If I wanted wood carvings, I used Ira Spector. If I wanted murals on the walls, I used Hans and Betsy. They're great artists. We used really great people. Hans and Betsy were in Chicago. They met in Chicago because he was a teacher at the Chicago Art Institute. They then made a living as artists, basically selling their works in department stores and that sort of thing. They moved to New Mexico, where they did a lot of work for years, where they got to meet Georgia O'Keeffe. In the 1950s, they came to Los Angeles and did work for Armet & Davis.

Q: How did they work together when you were working with them at Armet & Davis?

VN: They were doing a lot of the stuff in the Bob's Big Boys. Basically, working with Helen, who wanted a screen here, they wanted some artwork on the back walls. For that order they decided what kind of artwork. Then we used to use the stained glass. We're talking about Bob's now. I remember designing the chandeliers myself. Then we would have them constructed by Fred Glassman. We do the door pulls. We did the whole damn thing. The clocks. We didn't screw around.

Q: Total design. So you were happy working with them. You didn't have to direct them too much. They would get the sense of what was needed.

VN: It was a team, yeah. You work with them. They would come in. We would have meetings. We would talk about it. They would have designs.

Q: Who were some of the other artists?

VN: Roger Darricarrere. He was very good at stained glass. Then we used to have people who did our light fixtures. Fred Glassman was an example. Everything was custom. We did nothing but custom at the time. We had a lot of other artists. Bijan Shokatfard was another one. He was a metal sculptor.

Q: So the project designer would say, "We need a piece of art here"?

VN: Right. "We need a mural. We need this. We need that." When I did a lot of work for Miami International Airport, I [worked with an artist named] Barbara Trotter. She had a stable of artists and produced all of our work. It had to be a theme. As an example, if it was a Norm's building, if you want a mural on a wall, we would take about a 20-foot wall or 30-foot wall and just do it.

Q: Like the one at Norm's La Cienega?

VN: La Cienega would be an example. I didn't have anything to do with La Cienega, obviously. It was before my time, but that's the way we would do things.

A lot of these artists, like I said, came from Europe. A lot of them escaped. Roger Darricarrere was in the Resistance in World War II. To be honest with you, Hans Werner left because he was a communist. Well, socialist. Pretty much, I would say a communist. We didn't care what they were. All we cared about was getting the work done.

He had to leave [Europe], in fact. He had an interesting story. He was doing a mural in Munich. He was up on a scaffold inside a bureau or a public building. He said, "I was up there, I was doing my painting, and my boss comes down and he says, 'Come down. I want you to meet somebody.'" So [Hans] climbs down off the ladder and he's being introduced to Adolf Hitler. He said he had to shake hands with Hitler, I swear to God. Hans said, "I knew when I did that, I had to get the hell out of the country." So he tried to figure out a way to leave.

He said it was like a coin flip for him, to go either to Argentina or the United States. He figured he wouldn't last much longer if he continued to stay. I never knew if he was Jewish or not. Some people that we did deal with were, so that was the reason to leave. I think in his particular case, it might've been in politics. He remembered getting on the boat to the United States. He said he noticed that the third class was completely full of Jews leaving the country. He said, Boy, he knew the country was in real trouble. He went first class. He says, "If I'm going to leave, I'm going to go first class." So he left first class. Well, he said it was first class or second class. God knows what, but that's how he came into the United States, as a teacher.

Q: Then he taught at the Chicago Art Institute. It was a very distinguished place.

You have a panel by Hans where he captures the mid-century aesthetic with modern gears, plastic, and metal and found pieces in an abstract composition. Was his earlier work more traditional?

VN: I don't think they were ever traditional, because I have some of his work, which I would consider Brutalist. His work, [Betsy's] work, which I consider better, I'd never part with them. Betsy signed [her work in a way] so that they wouldn't know she was a woman.

Q: Are they watercolor?

VN: No, they're oils and they're abstract.

Q: The artists must have appreciated your commercial projects to help support their careers.

VN: Yeah. We'd make the clients pay for the fees.

Q: Why did you go to that effort? Why even have art?

VN: Why? Come on. The buildings had to have art. The buildings were art and they're not going to be completed.... If you take a look at the original Clock restaurant design interiors, they didn't look that great. The exterior looked great. The interior didn't. You needed somebody like Helen Fong, who had that feeling that you wanted something different inside. You didn't want to just copy some other stuff that had been produced by some other architects, some other place. [You wanted it] for a reason, though. We wanted something that was eye-catching and nice.

Q: One thing that has made this book possible is the fact that you have saved all of these drawings. This is just incredible. A lot of architects toss their old stuff. Why have you saved this, and what does it mean to you or to anybody else, do you think?

VN: Nothing to anybody else, maybe. But for me, I realized that we had all these renderings, and I decided to have them framed and saved. I figured that would be the best way. So I took the best renderings and saved them.

Q: One more question I want you to think about. In the early '60s, you were at the center of Southern California Modernism. Abell, Quincy Jones, Armet & Davis. I'd like you to tell us what that was like. The designs were so incredible. Nothing like it going on anywhere else in the country.

VN: We never looked at it that way. It was just what you did. This is how you made a living. I mean, OK, we saw a lot of architecture that wasn't good. But we knew we were good. The people that I was working for were the best, and I was learning. It was a learning process for me. I expected to learn. I was going to graduate school with these guys. This is all I cared about. I wanted the experience and to have the knowledge. So there you are.

ACKNOWLEDGMENTS

Victor Newlove, Danny King, Tony Wurman, Fred Davis, Sara Crown, Zoë Poledouris Roché, Ed Ruscha, the Ed Ruscha office, Angel City Press, Eldon Davis, Helen Fong, Chris Nichols, Adriene Biondo, John English, Peter Moruzzi, Sian Winship, Sven Kirsten, the Los Angeles Conservancy.

PROJECT INDEX

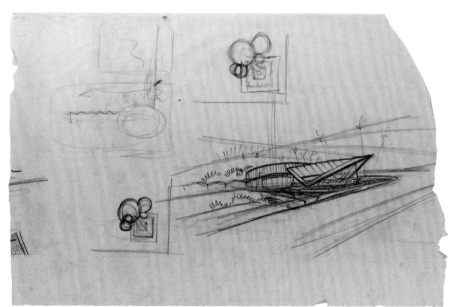

Untitled study, c. 1957